FREE AT LAST

Phillip E. Kenney

GLOSSARY

Agnostic - Someone who says we cannot know whether God exists

Apocrypha - A section of the Bible not accepted by all Christians.

Atheist - Someone who does not believe there is a God.

Communion - The most important of the Christian services. It acts out the events of the Last Supper, which Jesus had with his disciples.

Christ - the English word for the Hebrew word Messiah. It is not the surname of Jesus, as surnames were just coming into use during Jesus' time. However, surnames were used to further identify somebody who had a common first name.

Disciple - A person who follows the teachings of Jesus.

Epistle - A letter. Many epistles were written to the churches by Paul.

Epiphany - to make known a realization of truth.

Gospel - The part of the New Testament about the life of Jesus. Gospel means 'good news.'

Grace - The loving help that God gives to all human beings, an undeserved gift.

Jesus Christ - Name and title of the Son of God. Jesus is the English form of the Hebrew Yehoshua. It means the Lord saves. His mother called him Yeshua.

Meek - does not mean weak; it means mild, even-tempered, modest, peaceable, and gentle.

Messiah - Jesus of Nazareth is the Messiah, which means 'King' or 'Savior' or 'Anointed One'.

Trinity - The three natures of God in one being: The Father, the Son, and the Holy Spirit.

Rapture - To be 'caught up' and taken away to heaven.

Reconciliation - Made right by Jesus' death, we are reconciled to God. **Secular** - Not believing in God, the supernatural, or any existence beyond this physical life. The world is secular.

World - Describes the social order of humankind that is opposed and separated from the spiritual. Also includes false gods. Satan is the god of this world.

PREFACE

The truth shall make you free. However, there can be no freedom without justice and righteousness. The world seeks peace and freedom but insists on denying the truth. For them to accept the truth, they have to accept God, the giver of truth. This would require them to live by the rules of God, which they refuse to do. These devotions in *Free at Last* will guide sincere seekers in discovering the giver of truth, that truth is absolute, and ultimately, peace and freedom will follow.

This book consists of eighty-four daily devotions covering a period of 12 weeks. It is designed for use by those transitioning from incarceration back into society while maintaining their Christian faith. This process is to be supported by a trained mentor, who will also follow along in the devotions, help with prayers, explanations, making plans, and general accountability. As it says in many ads, "Serious Enquiries Only." Do not use this series as a mechanism to escape or avoid the consequences of bad behavior. This is intended only for those who seriously want to change their behavior and find a new life. It is assumed that these devotions will be read by the protégé and become a catalyst for discussion with a mentor, assisting in both growth and accountability.

We often refer to recovery or rehabilitation. These terms assume there was once a life worth recovering. The truth is that many people have lived in a constant state of dysfunction and never enjoyed either peace or freedom from the clutches of the enemy. The truth of God is the only way to live in peace and harmony with Him and others. It is sincerely desired that this devotional series will lead to God those who have spent their lives in chaos and disaster, and they will find them to be a source of His truth leading to the abundant life He makes possible.

INTRODUCTION

Many of the devotions in this book were originally published in *The Walk* by Mountain Christian Church in Joppa, MD, for use in their Small Group Ministry. Many parts of the text from *The Walk* have been revised and are used herein with permission. The revised text and other devotions are intended to help men and women as they endeavor to continue in their Christian faith while they transition from incarceration back into the community. However, others will also find it useful in their search for truth and living a life in a relationship with God.

Because you are reading this book, you have taken the initial step of seeking to know what is true about the universe and human endeavors. You have embarked on a journey, a search to find the truth, whether God exists, who He is, and what this means about the way you should live. The devotions and the questions are intended to change your way of thinking. If your thought process remains the same, nothing else will change, so you must open up to new patterns of thought. This can be a frightening prospect since your life has been based on self instead of the presence of a living and faithful God. You are to be congratulated for taking this important step that a great many people avoid.

If you are genuinely seeking to know the truth, this search will lead you into a life of joy, confidence, and peace about the future. Knowing the real truth and living accordingly will help you avoid many troubles in life, but it will also be a means to carry you through the troubles that are sure to come. When you rely on the truth, you will find that troubles make you a stronger person instead of overwhelming you. You no longer need to worry about your eternal destiny because you will come to realize that as a child of God you continue your relationship with Him throughout this life on earth and on for eternity.

Although the principle topics in this book are presented in a somewhat necessary chronological order of understanding, you will find that you also have to work on all of them at the same time. The topics are interrelated, and some ideas are repeated in subsequent devotionals. These topics are not something you are likely to grasp in a single reading, so take your time and meditate on them. Now, let's proceed to the beginning, knowing that God is, and what you need to do as a result of this knowledge.

If you are not familiar with the Bible, you may want to visit Appendix II. It will give you a brief introduction that will help in finding the Scripture references in this study.

Table of Contents

STUDY 1 - TRUTH

Day 1 - The Search
Read: John 1:17-18

Before we can become "Free at Last," we must know what is true and what is false. Everyone has an opinion about the truth. But you need to find out for yourself what is true. In courtrooms and science classes, in poetry books and newspapers, in politics and in religion, people are making their own claims about truth. Some are foolish enough to profess that nothing is true, that all things are relative. Christians also make some pretty amazing claims about what is true. In this study series, we will begin our search for truth with the Bible, whether we can trust it to be true, and whether it is a reliable guide for our lives.

You may wonder why the Bible should be chosen for the start of our search. The Bible is one of the oldest and most universal books, claiming to be true and containing the very words of God. We need to know whether we can believe this audacious claim or whether we should dismiss it and look elsewhere.

Our culture has made it easy to have a casual attitude about truth. We choose a side with which we are comfortable and that we consider trustworthy. Then, we assume those on the other side are trying to deceive us. Unfortunately, we let our moral values get in the way of an objective decision. All too often we avoid making any choices at all, only to find we have simply drifted through our lives and missed the chance to live the abundant life. You can begin to make up for this casual way of life by deciding to investigate, to ask, to think, and to question. You may have come from a religious background that discouraged questions, or you may have no religious background at all. You will be challenged by this study to pursue the truth. Asking questions of God and of Scripture is exactly what is required for those who would faithfully follow Jesus and the Bible. The truth has nothing to fear.

In this pursuit, you will be encouraged to seek out the Bible and try to understand its meanings. You will need to question to use your mind and reasoning powers to decide who can be trusted and what can be known. You will need to examine your experience and the experiences of others. You can be sure that many others have done the same and have not failed to find what they were seeking. Never fear that the pursuit of truth will lead you astray, for God is the source of all that is true.

Jesus said, "If you hold to my teaching, you are really my disciples. Then you will know the truth, and the truth will set you free."
John 8:31–32

Every day all of us have to make decisions about what is true and whom to trust. We are influenced by science, parents, friends, school, media, government, the church as well as our personal experiences. But how can we know whether we are getting the truth from these sources? First and foremost, you will need to put away any personal biases and prejudice. You must be willing to open your mind and sincerely search to learn what is true and reasonable. It is a paradox that Christians are accused of having their minds closed when, in fact, one has to have an open mind to learn the truth. But that mind then has to use the truth to filter out the junk (untruth) that is constantly shoved in our faces by the so-called "enlightened" social order.

God is a God of Truth and so we have nothing to fear from seeking truth. We are invited to pursue truth. We do not need to be afraid to come to Scripture and ask honest questions. The Bible is a strong book; it can handle our questions. The search for the truth is always a search in the right direction. Confidence in the truth of the Bible is foundational to living in the footsteps of Christ. Therefore, we should never ignore our honest questions, nor should we be afraid to take a stand on what we have come to believe. This is your opportunity to clarify your position as a pursuer of truth. None of us has arrived. All of us can continue to seek the truth about Jesus and the Bible.

Questions and activities:

1. According to Jesus, how important is the search for truth?

2. What do you believe is the meaning of life?

3. What is missing in your life?

4. Do you know of any other religious faith that encourages searching for answers?

5. What questions do you need to have answered before you can accept this truth? Write them here and discuss them with your mentor later.

Day 2 - Healthy Doubt
Read: John 20:24–31

"I just can't do it!" I shouted as I stormed inside the house. We had finally mounted our new basketball hoop in the garage. My older brother and I had long anticipated this day. With a new basketball and a new goal, we went out to the driveway and began to shoot (and, in my case, miss) baskets. I am sure that I didn't miss every shot, but that is how I remember it. Shot after shot, I missed. My lay-ups bounced off the rim. My jump shots fell short or bounced off the garage roof. I left the driveway convinced that I was incapable of making a basket.

"I can do it," I insisted as I reached up to remove the burnt-out light bulb.

"It'll be hot," my cousin warned.

"I can take it," I replied.

I unscrewed the light bulb and stepped down from the chair. The heat registered, and I dropped the light bulb. It shattered. We went to find a broom and dustpan.

In both cases, I was wrong. When I concluded that I just couldn't play basketball, what I really needed was practice and patience. When I was sure that I could handle the light bulb, I set myself up for failure. I bounce back and forth between those extremes a lot. In my ignorance, I often assume I have all the answers and, if I don't, that I can figure them out on my own. When I meet resistance or struggle, I am often quick to give up and accept defeat. Many people have chosen one of these extremes regarding truth. They either assume they know it all, or they are sure they can't know anything. Instead of honestly seeking, they have decided that they will never know the truth. They have concluded that perhaps no one can ever know. You may be in this place. You may once have wondered if the Bible was true or if miracles really happened. Perhaps you have given up wondering and walked away from the pursuit of truth by throwing up your hands and concluding, "We'll never know." Or, perhaps, you think you have all the answers. Human nature often drives us to believe this lie. Many of the conversations that happen even within the church are merely arguments between those who insist they have all the answers. They think they know all there is to know simply because they have decided to stop asking questions. Likewise, many dismiss the claims of Jesus and the Bible not because they have investigated these claims and found them lacking, but because they decided in advance never to ask the questions.

God desires you to ask questions and continually seek after the truth. To walk after Christ, you must pursue the truth. It is not acceptable to decide that you know everything, nor should you decide that you are not capable of knowing. Neither option is sufficient. These are the fundamental questions of life. These questions demand a search. The decision to keep seeking within Scripture and its teaching is essential. It is a huge decision for your faith and for your walk with Christ. The quest for truth matters. What we all need is healthy doubt. That may sound surprising, so let me clarify. We need to go to God and God's Word with seeking hearts and minds. We need to ask the questions and do the work to find the answers without trying to confirm what we already believe.

The apostle Thomas is almost always labeled a "doubter." But this label misses the strength of his character. He does doubt, but his doubt leads him toward a quest for truth. He is not content in his doubt; he is not arrogant in mistaken assurance. He asks questions. Asking questions is healthy. In fact, the author tells us that his message was written so that we might know what happened, test the evidence, and make a judgment about its truth. John, the author, is specifically encouraging us to bring our doubts to Christ, just as Thomas did. We cannot touch the hands, but we can test the evidence.

Questions:

1. Have you ever found that something you believe was actually not true? How did this affect you?

2. Do you believe there is truth that you have yet to discover?

3. What questions and doubts do you have about Jesus?

4. What about the story of Jesus do you find most difficult to accept?

5. Discuss your questions and doubts with your mentor.

Day 3 - Fact or Opinion
Read: John 14:1-11

The tomato is the tastiest vegetable of them all. The previous sentence is a truth claim. This type of claim makes a statement about the way things are. It can be argued and defined; it can be denied or agreed upon. You may have already reacted to the fact that tomatoes are the tastiest vegetable of them all. Perhaps you disagree. Perhaps you are a fan of snow peas, fresh from the garden, sweet and crunchy. Maybe you love zucchini. It is so versatile; it can be stir-fried, deep-fried, and baked. It can be made into bread and cookies. In this case, you would not call the opening sentence a lie. Some of you wouldn't even say it was wrong.

You would just disagree.

Perhaps you know that the tomato is not scientifically a vegetable at all. It is a fruit. In this case, you could refer to a commonly accepted set of standards that define what is a fruit and what is a vegetable. You would say that the above truth claim is not merely one with which you disagree. It's just plain wrong. In this case, one person's opinion about taste is not the issue at all. Instead, the issue is a question of botanical definition. The tomato is botanically a fruit, and even if I say otherwise, that doesn't change what the word "fruit" means or what a tomato is.

Let's try another more serious claim: Jesus Christ is the Son of God. The previous sentence is also a claim about truth. It is a statement about the way things are. This is the question: "Is this claim more like saying that tomatoes are tasty, or more like the claim that tomatoes are a vegetable?" There was a time when it was assumed that religious claims were more like the claims about fruit. They made statements about the way things really were. When I say that the tomato is a fruit, I am claiming something about the real structure of tomato plants. Similarly, when Christians claimed that Jesus was the Son of God, people assumed that was a claim about the true nature of a man who once lived.

7

However, many disagreed with this claim. Many thought this claim was foolishness and a falsehood. But no one imagined that Jesus being the Son of God could be true for some and not true for others! No one imagined that it was a matter of personal taste and not a claim about the way things really are. In the last 30 years, this has changed. More and more people assume that religious claims are more like the claims about a tomato's tastiness than its botany. In fact, many people have begun to assume that most truth claims are matters open to disagreement rather than a judgment of what is true or false. Unlike botany, in matters of faith, commonly accepted standards have broken down so that many people find themselves unable or unwilling to judge between the truth claims of different faiths. It has become an easy excuse to believe that religious ideas may be true for one person but not for another. In this understanding, religious views do not make claims about reality but instead merely reveal opinions and points of view. They can be disagreed with (just as you would disagree about the tastiest vegetable), but they cannot be argued based on evidence.

Jesus did not intend for those who encountered Him to have this way of escape. In John 14:6, again, we encounter Thomas asking Jesus to know the way to God's house. Jesus replied, "I am the way and the truth and the life. No one comes to the Father except through me." Jesus was aware of the truth claims of other religions. His words are stark and even harsh in their exclusivity. Jesus claims that other ways are wrong and this way is right. You can disagree with Jesus. You are free to conclude that He is wrong or mistaken about His own significance in the world. Please do not, however, commit the intellectual dishonesty of assuming that the claims of Christ and the church are matters of taste.

Questions:

1. Many people believe that Jesus was a great moral teacher who taught many good things for us to follow. How do you know what is good to follow and what is not?

2. What do you see wrong with a great moral teacher making the claims Jesus made?

3. In what way is refusing to accept Jesus the same as rejecting Him?

4. What do you see different about Jesus' teaching and the teaching of the other world religions?

5. Why can't religious belief be just a matter of personal opinion?

Day 4 - Testing the Truth
Read: Matthew 9:1-8

There is an art to lying. I am sad to say that I know this largely from personal experience. A good lie needs to be believable but not testable or verifiable. It must have enough details so that it sounds like a real story, but details must be of the sort that can never be tested or tried. For instance, "I once rode in a car at 145 miles per hour" is hard to verify, but it is so vague that it is neither believable nor compelling.

"David and I drove his new Civic at 145 miles per hour on I-95 last Friday" has plenty of compelling details but is easily verifiable. What if someone listening knows David? They could check the story and the game is up. I also have some skepticism about the ability of a Civic to sustain 145 miles per hour!

A better option might be, "When I visited my cousin's friend in West Virginia, he had this old Mustang. He had just put a new engine in it and wanted to test it out. We went out driving, and on the way back, he broke 150 on a straight section of highway." Told in this way and with enough emotion, the lie is easy to believe and impossible to verify. Even if some skeptics were to doubt your word, are they willing to drive to West Virginia and check? A good lie is one that deflects criticism from the start.

Many texts of the world's religions have a lot in common with such artful stories. They have tenuous connections with historical facts. They tell stories that cannot be independently verified or contradicted. They claim mystical truths and tell of events that happen in other worlds or in the realm of the gods. They may be true, but none of our common tools for determining truth will help in proving these stories to be true.

Unlike Greek mythology or other stories with gods, the truths of Christian Scripture are completely different. They arise from stories and records that are absolutely historical. Christ models this reality in one of His most dramatic encounters with potential skeptics. The

Bible text listed above is a story recorded in three gospels, and I think I know why. It is fantastic! Jesus begins by making a sweeping but highly spiritual claim. It is powerful and specific but cannot be verified by anyone present. It is the perfect lie. The skeptics scoff and accuse him of blasphemy. He does not bluster or boast. In some sense, He honors their skepticism and does something they never suspected. He heals the man. This they can verify. This they can see. This is no lie. The false healer diagnoses and cures an illness that no one else can test. Jesus invites a man they knew to be lame to arise and walk. Jesus does not want to be believed because He is a smooth talker and can outwit the other teachers of the day. He backs up what He teaches. He wants His words and His teaching to be tested because He knows that they will prove true.

Ultimately, this is true of the entire Christian faith. The central Christian truth claim is not a theological idea or a moral code. The center of Christian truth is that a man who lived in history truly died and truly rose again. He did not just appear to be dead; he was crucified, stabbed and buried for three days. Guards were placed at the tomb to prevent deception. Nevertheless, He arose and was seen alive again by more than 500 people (John 19–21). His followers didn't make up the story but had trouble believing it themselves. The center of Christian truth is that a man who lived in history truly died and truly rose again. Just as with the lame man, Jesus does not want us to stumble while mulling over the value of His moral code. Rather, the value of the moral code rests on His resurrection. If you want to investigate the truth of Christianity, you would be wise to start at the center. Christianity was never intended to be a good lie. If it is a lie, it is a very bad lie because the whole matter rests on a remarkably unlikely historical claim: that a man named Jesus died and rose again.

This is the center. Test this. Study the alternatives. Ask hard questions. If it did not happen, then Christians are most to be pitied (1 Corinthians 15:19). But if Christ did rise from the dead, then grace is real, God is real, forgiveness is real and death is defeated!

Questions:

1. Christianity is a historical faith not because it is old but because it is rooted in claims about historical events. How does this open the faith up to a variety of attacks on its truth?

2. What historical claims of the Bible would you like to investigate?

3. Does it encourage you to know that, like the lame man walking, the truths of Scripture can be tested and verified?

4. Do you question the truth about Alexander the Great or Plato? Would it surprise you to know that the evidence for the life and teaching of Jesus is far more reliable than it is for any other historical character?

5. How much proof do you need to believe in God and salvation through Jesus?

Day 5 - Reliability of the Records
Read: Luke 1:1-4

The internet has changed the way I approach what is true and what is false. A friend sent me a web link that really upset her.

She wrote, "I never knew any of this." I followed the link, and my thought was, "I don't believe any of this, either."

After a half-hour of research, it was clear that the author was ill-informed and wrong.

I finally wrote back to my friend with this response: "The reason you never knew any of that is because it isn't true. Remember, with the internet, you have to know who wrote it. Don't believe everything you read."

There are some websites that, over time, you learn are trustworthy. They check sources and validate posts. But, unless you know the site is reliable, you must be very careful about what you read on the internet.

I never did that with my school textbooks. I remember when I first read about the Trail of Tears and the cruel way that Native Americans were treated as Europeans settled in the Americas.

I thought to myself, "This is outrageous; I never heard any of this." However, I did not look to see who wrote the book or track down the publisher to check if they were reliable or not. I trusted the book because I trusted the context in which I received the book. I knew that it had been approved by knowledgeable and trustworthy teachers and scholars. In particular, I had teachers who had studied the topic, and I could trust them to correct any errors in the textbook. As I assessed the reliability of the text, knowing the context of what was being taught was even more important than knowing the identity of the author. As we turn to Scripture and try to determine its reliability, we face many of the same issues. Where did these books come from? Can I trust the author? Are these random words from the pages of history, or is there some reason to trust their contents?

Most of the Bible is anonymous. Consequently, how can we know that it was not fabricated? As a teen, I had one recurring, nagging doubt. Could the whole thing have been made up by a small group of people sometime in the first or second century? Was this all a great hoax? What I have come to know since then is that the reliability of Scripture lies not in its authorship but rather in the context of its creation. We don't believe it because we know who wrote it but because we know who first read it. Its authority rests not on the memory and inspiration of one person but on the collective memory and wisdom of God's people. As an example, consider the first four books of the New Testament. The books, called gospels, are short biographies of the life of Jesus. The four Gospels of the New Testament were all anonymous writings. In the texts themselves, none of them make any claims of authorship. The common titles (Matthew, Mark, Luke, and John) are the designations of tradition and are not identified in the texts themselves. Therefore, the foundation of reliability is not based on the authors. The foundation is the church. When these books were written, the church existed. As the four gospels were written and distributed, there were eyewitnesses alive in the church who could say, "Yes, that is how it happened." Second-generation Christians could say to one another, "I have always loved that story. I remember when Peter visited our church and talked about that same thing."

In contrast, it is popular today to talk about "lost" gospels, like the recently rediscovered "Gospel of Judas." This term often implies that these authoritative works were misplaced over the course of history. They were not misplaced; they were ignored, and for good reason. Imagine for a moment that in the second century, someone wrote a gospel and began to distribute it. If it told stories about Jesus that no one had ever heard, the church would quickly recognize that it simply wasn't true. So, it would have been forgotten and ignored. In contrast, those gospels that were written early, while first and second-generation Christians were alive and able to validate their reliability, were copied distributed, and shared.

The criteria for accepting a new gospel were not complicated. Many who were alive had witnessed the original events. Many more were alive who had been taught by the eyewitnesses. These people could read a first edition of Matthew or a copy of Luke when it was delivered to their church and judge on a most simple set of criteria. "Yep, that's the way it happened. Read it to the kids and make a Xerox copy so we never forget."

Questions:

1. Have you ever heard anybody criticize a book or movie when they never read it or seen it?

2. Is it dishonest for somebody to claim the Bible is false if they have never read it?

3. Is there anything that prevents you from reading through the Bible?

4. Did you know that some of the most famous critics of the Bible were converted to Christ while reading it to find the errors?

5. What would you say to a person who claims the Bible contradicts itself?

Day 6 - Life in the Word
Read: Genesis 2:1-15

The little pile of colored latex lay in his hand. It was nothing. Perhaps it was less than nothing. It was trash. Then, he began to pump air into one end. He twisted and turned and blew more air into the no longer formless blue latex. With a flourish, he held it out.

I exclaimed, "Look, it's a sword."

My son, apparently more religious than I, corrected me, "No, Daddy, it's a cross."

And so, it was. A little air and a few well-chosen twists and less than nothing turned into a child's delight. God took formless matter and gave it form. God molded the pieces together and shaped their structure. Then God came close to this lifeless form and breathed into it. This breath gave life and spirit to that which was once lifeless and devoid of spirit. Similar forms existed, but this one was different. It breathed with the breath of God.

This is the Bible's dramatic witness to the creation of people (Genesis 2; Ezekiel 37). All living things are formed from matter and shaped by God in the same way. I suppose it is not surprising that humans have much in common scientifically with many other animals. What sets humans apart is not the material of their making but the breath of God. This word, which we translate as "breath," is a powerful word in Hebrew. It is used to describe breath and wind and spirit and life itself.

So, God does not just put air in the lungs of humanity. God gives us spirit. We are alive in a way that all other living creatures are not. We are alive with the Spirit of God. Based upon this understanding of the creation of humanity, the apostle Paul writes something amazing to his young protégé, Timothy:

> *"All scripture is God-breathed and is useful for teaching,*
> *rebuking, correcting and training in righteousness, so that all*
> *God's people may be thoroughly equipped for every good work."*
> *2 Timothy 3:16–17*

According to Paul, the Bible's creation was infused with God's breath, just like human creation.

What was said about the creation of people is true about the creation of Scripture. The Bible has much in common with other books. It uses the language and expressions specific to its time period. It reflects a historical voice and composition. It was written on paper using the ink of its day. In these various ways, it is much like the other books of the period. But Paul identifies a singular distinction. This book is God-breathed. This word is often translated as "God-inspired." Even in English, we can see a reminder that to be "inspired" is to be "in-spirited." This is what Paul is trying to teach us. These particular pages and words were given to their creation, the Spirit of God. God has used the normal stuff of human writing: an author's memories, a community's songs, paper and ink. This is the same "ground" out of which all books come. But in the forming of this book, God was uniquely present. This is only the first half of the implication of Paul's teaching. The breath breathed into the creation of people was not just for their formation. It is the spirit and breath of life that makes us alive. In the same way, the Bible continues to be alive with God's breath. The author of Hebrews teaches us:

"For the word of God is alive and active. Sharper than any double-edged sword, it penetrates even to dividing soul and spirit, joints and marrow; it judges the thoughts and attitudes of the heart."

Hebrews 4:12

This is true of God's Word, spoken, preached, and written. This is true of the Bible. If the balloon loses its air, it is trash again. The Bible never loses its air. The Bible upholds the Christian faith not just because God breathed into its creation but also because this same breath still gives the Bible life.

The Bible upholds the Christian faith not just because God breathed into its creation but also because God's breath still gives the Bible life. Do not be afraid to expect big things from faithful Bible study. You are invited to investigate its pages and get to know its stories. You will be surprised by what you find. You will be surprised to find that it still breathes. Into your life, God's Word can breathe truth.

Questions:

1. Our society has forsaken the Word of God and grasped the theory of evolution to explain the origin of life without a life-giving being. What problems do you see with this theory?

2. In the second paragraph above, it says man is set apart from the animals by the breath of God. Think of at least five major differences you can see between man and the other creatures in nature.

3. God made us for fellowship with Him, but Adam chose to go his own way by his disobedience to God's commands. What has God done to restore our broken relationship with Him?

4. In what ways are you different from Adam?

5. What happens when you lose your air?

Day 7 - Trust the Guide Book
Read: Psalm 23

The Appalachian Trail Association publishes a series of trail guides for the entire Appalachian Trail. They are essential volumes for anyone wanting to understand the Appalachian Trail or to research the phenomenon of hiking in America. However, that is not their purpose. These guides are designed to be carried while you hike. They are light and small. They contain the history of the trail and talk about its construction. The guides will often comment on others' experiences with a particular trail. They give information about the glorious views and the difficult climbs. The guides tell where healthy springs can be found and which springs seem beautiful, but whose water would make you sick if it is not boiled first. In sections where bears are common, the warnings are repeated often. Shelters and trail crossings are clearly marked so that you can plan your hike. The guides also tell you how to get on the trail at various locations and how to pace yourself so that you can finish the hike. It does not try to answer all the questions you might have. It is not a geology book, but it will mention rocks if a warning about a rocky trail section would be helpful. In particular, it has all the information that you would need to get on the trail and hike, nothing more and nothing less.

Thinking about a trail guide helps me to understand what Paul is trying to teach Timothy when he describes the Bible as "useful." He writes that Scripture is "useful for teaching, rebuking, correcting and training in righteousness, so that the person of God may be thoroughly equipped for every good work." The usefulness that Paul describes is a lot like the usefulness of a trail guide. God wants to walk in a relationship with you. God, through Christ, has blazed a trail for you. On the pages of Scripture, you will find everything that is needed for you to understand how to join the walk and stay on the trail, as well as what you can expect to see along the way. There is history so that you can read the stories and understand the struggles of how the trail was made and who has walked before you. There is poetry to give you a glimpse of the joy, sorrow, praise, and even the doubt you might experience as you walk. There are warning signs for danger and for springs that are poisonous. And there is guidance toward unexpected joys and streams of living water. The Bible answers many of life's questions, but it is not an answer book. Many questions remain unanswered. It is a trail guide, and it gives us enough so that we can trust the trailblazer and follow in His footsteps, nothing more and nothing less.

Like the trail guide, people may read the Bible for other reasons. Researchers interested in understanding first-century religious experience can read the Bible as a sourcebook. Theologians can read the Bible to better understand the complex nature of God's character. These readings are helpful and positive. But they are not what the Bible is for. This is a book of action. The truth of Scripture makes you look for boots and a backpack to begin hiking to this new adventure.

Questions:

1. Would you start out on a journey without checking maps and getting the latest information you would need?

2. What kind of information would you look for if you were going on a hike?

3. What would you say to people who have no knowledge of the Bible but say it is not relevant to today?

4. In addition to the Bible, what two other sources of direction are available to help you along the trail of life?

5. What is it about God that gives you confidence in His leadership?

6. How would you feel living with a religion that teaches you only to follow the rules and doesn't offer a relationship with God?

Other Reading: Pilgrim's Progress by John Bunyon

STUDY 2 – GRACE

Day 1 – God's Love
Read: John 3:16-17; Romans 5:6–8

> *"You see, at just the right time, when we were still powerless,*
> *Christ died for the ungodly. Very rarely will anyone die for a*
> *righteous person, though for a good person, someone might*
> *possibly dare to die. But God demonstrates his own love for us in*
> *this: While we were still sinners, Christ died for us."*
> *Romans 5:6-8*

We are prone to say things like, "I just loved that book" or, "I would love to go on a cruise," but our use of the word love in these instances is not the same as when we say, "I love my mother." When I say, "I love my mother," it isn't exactly the same as when I say, "I love my wife." The English language lacks the words to express these feelings of emotion adequately. On the other hand, we are also equally careless in our use of words to exactly express these emotions. Until we understand the various forms of love, we are unable to comprehend or accept the depths of God's love. We will continue to struggle with believing God truly loves us through all circumstances. Often, we ask how He can allow us to suffer as we do if He truly loves us and is capable of our rescue.

One day, I was preparing to let my dog out through the sliding glass door. I knew when I opened the door, he would bolt through the opening. I could also see that the screen door was pulled shut, and he would crash into it. I made him sit and stay until I could open the door and pull the screen out of the way. Just like us waiting for God, I am sure my dog did not understand why he was made to sit and stay, but God can foresee our circumstances. He knows what is best for us, even if it means delays or emotional suffering. You see, He knows what we will have to pass through. None of us will get out of this life alive. We all came with a lifetime guarantee but we don't know how long that will be. I like to use the relationship we have with our pets to help us understand the concept of a loving, all-knowing (omniscient) God.

This week, we will examine the most basic of Christian claims: that God's love for us precedes our turning to Him. Before we consider even one of the steps that we are called to take in following Christ, we need to understand God's grace and His love for us. God's love, although similar to that of a parent's love for a child, goes far beyond parental love. The Greek word for God's kind of love is "Agape." It means that we are loved even though we are undeserving. We are loved unconditionally. God didn't love us because we were obedient to Him but loved in spite of our disobedience. Jesus said, "Greater love has no one than this, that he lay down his life for his friends." Yet, as you can see from the text you read above, Christ died for us, not because we were His friends, but before we were willing to acknowledge Him.

Nothing we can ever do or say or think or experience; no piece of our past or present or future can change God's love for us. To love someone, to truly love someone, is to make a commitment to pursue that person's best interests. The Creator has made this commitment toward all of creation. Every action God has taken has been out of love for us and for the entire world. "Truth" was the first leg in our walk with Christ, "grace" is the second. No meaningful step in following Jesus is taken apart from his love and grace.

Questions:

1. How does it make you feel to know that the Creator of the universe knows you and loves you even though you are undeserving?

2. Knowing that God loves you unconditionally, are you willing to trust Him in all areas of your life?

3. God loves you too much to leave you the way you are. What areas do you have trouble giving up to Him?

4. Do you see God's grace in Islam, Hinduism, Buddhism, or any other religious teaching?

5. How would you describe "grace" in relationship to "love?"

Day 2 – Just Receive
Read: 2 Kings 5:1-15

I understand Naaman. I suffer from the twin sins of arrogance and doubt. These may seem like unlikely twins to you, but inside, they are very similar. Arrogance says that I believe I can do and understand anything. Doubt says that anything that I cannot do or understand, I will not believe. Like Naaman, most of us know that we are not yet what we want to be. You may even have the mysterious feeling that you are not yet what you were meant to be. I have had this feeling and I have gone to many "kings" looking to be healed or fixed or fulfilled. None of them were as humble as the king of Israel. The kings of academics, consumption, wealth, and family were all sure that they could satisfy. But they did not. Perhaps you as well, have gone to these with your hurt and dissatisfaction and found their promises unreliable. If that is the case, I will not blame you if you are skeptical when you hear how the King of Kings, the Creator God, offers to heal you and make you whole. I will understand if you, like Naaman, want to walk away instead of following Christ on the walk. Like dipping in a dirty river, God's plan to heal you is surprising in its simplicity. God's action on your behalf overturns our expectations.

This is what God proposes. God intends to release you from your burden of past mistakes. God intends to empower you to live as you were intended. God intends to secure for you a future in which you will be completely whole. And God intends for all of this to be a gift.

Naaman wanted to be cured. He was eager for Elijah to provide a way. Perhaps a way in which he could prove he was worthy to be healed. Maybe that is what you want from God. You may admit that you are a bit bent but insist you're not broken. You want a chance to make the cut so that God will reward you with restoration. Your question to God may be, "What work can I do to earn my healing?" The way Elijah provided was not what Naaman wanted. He could have washed in rivers on his own. Did Elijah really think that he hadn't already tried a good bath to cure his disease? His arrogance began to stand in the way of his healing. His doubt affected him as well. Was he really to believe that he could be healed so simply? It was too much to ask. The way that God has provided to you is also surprisingly simple. All those things that God proposes to do: to release you, to empower you, to secure your future, God intends to give you through the work of Christ that you accept in faith.

Grace is the undeserved gift of God's love. Love is God's choice to seek out your best good, no matter what sacrifice or action this requires. God has chosen to heal you. This is the message of the cross. God will do what it takes to reconcile and redeem creation. God loves us, though we don't deserve it, and this love is made clear in God's commitment to act in our best good no matter what. Elijah never told Naaman why this action would heal him. But Naaman's wise servant told him to do it anyway. Likewise, the Bible never fully explains why Jesus had to die to restore us. But we are told that:

"God so loved the world that he gave his one and only Son, that whoever believes in him shall not perish but have eternal life. For God did not send his Son into the world to condemn the world, but to save the world through him."
John 3:16,17

Christ has accomplished God's desire that a way of healing might be found for all of us. I will understand if you are tempted to arrogance or doubt. I still am sometimes, too. But I know that no other king can offer this healing.

Questions:

1. What was it about Naaman that made him angry and would have prevented him from being healed?

2. What did Naaman do that makes you suspect that he didn't understand grace?

3. In what way are you like Naaman?

4. Do you have somebody to stand beside you as Naaman's servant stood by him?

5. It is apparent that Naaman believed he could be healed. Do you have faith to receive the forgiveness and new life that God offers you through Jesus?

Day 3 – Grace in Action
Read: Mathew 20:1-16

This is a parable of grace. When the landowner pays the workers, grace is evident. The landowner does not pay according to what the workers deserve but according to his generosity. But that is not the primary act of grace in this text. Listen to this story retold from another perspective.

The old woman and the young boy sat in the dust, leaning against the fence that separated the road from the empty town square. They almost never spoke, but they had become friends bound by the same desperate hope. Neither should have been there, and both knew it was useless to stay, but neither would leave until the shadows got long enough to signal the end of the day. She was there because her husband had died, and she had no children; the boy was there because his father was sick, and his mother had to stay home to care for the rest of the family. Both had arrived early, hoping to be chosen, but by the time the landowners arrived, the square was full of strong, healthy men, ready and eager to work. A wagon pulled up, and the driver called out, "I need ten men to tend my vineyard." The woman and the boy had struggled to get in but were pushed back by the crowd. That was early in the morning, and now it was too late in the day; no one would hire them now. Together, they cursed their fate.

She thought, "Why has God let my husband die? Why does no one see me?"

He wondered, "Why is my father sick? Why must I be so weak— too weak to fight my way to the front of the line?"

The sun would set in an hour. They began to rise. They never spoke, but they both thought, "Another wasted day." However, as they rose, they heard a wagon coming toward town, probably workers returning a bit early. They kept walking.

From behind them, they heard the voice of the vineyard owner call out, "Why are you standing there doing nothing all day?" What a ridiculous question. He had been there several times that day already. He knew they wanted work but were too slow.

The old woman started to curse in reply, but in simple honesty, the boy spoke first, "Because no one has hired us."

Then the vineyard owner said to them, "Come with me to work in my vineyard." That's when grace happened. The amazing act of grace happens long before the vineyard owner breaks out the cash.

The first act of grace is when the landowner says, "Come be a part of my kingdom; be a worker in my house." Long before God's grace gives us paradise, it gives us purpose. Before we embrace the joy of heaven, Jesus has a job for us to do now. The first act of grace is God's invitation to us into the life intended for us. Paul tells us that we were orphans with no identity, hope, future, or parents. But now, because of grace, we are the children of God. Grace offers an identity change. It is the chance to be a part of something bigger than ourselves, bigger than any human endeavor. God has for each of us an abundant, purpose-filled life to be lived from now throughout eternity.

If you have accepted Christ, your eternal life has already begun.

Paul teaches that if anyone is in Christ, that person is a new creation. Eternal life is here. In the act of baptism our old self dies. That means the life we now live is our new life that will continue forever. Eternal life is now, so let's begin living that way. There are times when each of us feels like the old woman and the boy. We are sure that no one, least of all God, has anything for us. The first act of grace is God's invitation into the life God intended for us from the beginning of creation.

Questions:

1. How would you feel if you worked the whole day in the field and got paid the same as those who worked only one hour?

2. What would you say to those who only worked one hour?

3. How would you feel if you got paid a day's wage and worked only the last hour?

4. What would you say to those who complained about the pay?

5. How do you think this applies to receiving eternal life?

Day 4 – Bitterness
Read: Ephesians 4:17-32

In a sermon, our pastor told the story of a father who drank and was abusive to his two children, Mike and Emily. They would hide from him when he was drunk and had to wear long-sleeved shirts in the summertime to hide the bruises on their bodies from the violence they received at his hand. Later in life, their father died. Mike refused to attend his funeral because of his hatred and bitterness over the abuse. When Emily urged him to go with her, he accused her of being in denial. But she said, "I am not in denial. I am just not bitter like you are." She told Mike, "You know, you are becoming just as mean and stubborn and self-centered as our father was."

It is hard to discuss confession and forgiveness apart from the subject of bitterness. Bitterness is an irrational and devastating attitude that results from our failure to forgive. Carrying bitterness allows an offender to continue hurting us and leads to our own destruction. Usually, we will put the blame on the offender for the bitterness we carry, but bitterness is uniquely an offense we inflict on ourselves. Romans 3:14 uses bitterness in describing those under the power of sin. It is sin that causes the loss of many blessings of the normal Christian life, including emotional stability, peace, and joy.

In James 3:11-15 we are asked,

"Does the same spring produce both fresh and bitter water?"

What's more, bitterness is a foothold we give Satan to enter into our character. Our bitterness focuses our thoughts on the offender until we begin to take on the same character that we find so deplorable in them. Bitterness is a major contributing cause of other problems, including depression. What worse thing can we do to ourselves?

We cannot harbor a bitter spirit and maintain the healthy relationship God wants to have with us. We are bitter because we refuse to accept the wrong that has been done to us. We use that wrong to explain other events in our lives that are not to our satisfaction. We do this because we do not recognize that God is in control. Sometimes, we blame God for allowing things to go wrong rather than see these events as something He permits in order to develop our character.

Perhaps you have already allowed bitterness to reside in your life. As you read this, you are well aware of the devastating effects it has caused. So, you are asking, "What can be done about it?" In the next devotion, we will find that surrendering to God is the only way to overcome bitterness.

Questions:

1. What bitterness have you had or is currently troubling you?

2. What keeps you from giving up your bitterness?

3. When will you be ready to set this aside?

4. Do you think you can do this on your own?

5. Can you trust God to handle all the consequences?

Day 5 – Forgiveness
Read: Matthew 18:21-35; Mark 11:25

Forgiveness is the key to overcoming bitterness, anger, and rage.

God has given us the gift of forgiveness, demonstrated in the life of Christ. He has not only forgiven us but through His sacrifice, we are redeemed from eternal damnation. He expects us to show the same forgiveness to others. We are to forgive as we have been forgiven. As was said in yesterday's devotion, failure to forgive allows the devil a foothold in our lives. That foothold gives him the opportunity to lead us away from God and deeper into sin.

In the fallen state of mankind, forgiveness is not an action that is natural for us. We want to strike back at those who wrong us, but God says we are to be good to those who hurt us and use us. Following God's way has a supernatural element to it. When we forgive, it frees us from a heavy burden we are not equipped to handle. Harboring an offense can consume us emotionally, but forgiveness lifts a weight from our shoulders. Through forgiveness, we inherit a blessing. Forgiving turns the offense over to God, allowing Him to deal with it. He will work in ways we cannot imagine, either excusing or accusing the offender, even if they are not Christians. *"Vengeance is mine, says the Lord."* We can leave it up to Him instead of seeking to right the wrongs on our own. This is the secret to overcoming anger and rage in our lives and explains why so many people act hatefully!

I have met only a few people who are not carrying a burden of unforgiveness in their lives. Some are for very serious offenses and others minor. Sometimes, the offense was not even intentional or realized by the offender. How do we deal with forgiving someone who has hurt us? What do you do? Is there any hope? Forgiveness is much easier to say than to do. I know because I have been there.

The word "forgive" is a grace word in English as well as in Greek. An early meaning in English was "to give or to grant." Later, it came to mean "to remit a debt or to pardon an offense." God has forgiven all of us who are absolutely without resources of our own. He is not expecting or demanding some kind of payment in return for His grace gifts, but we are to be channels of grace to the world. A person who practices grace thinking (divine viewpoint) will become a forgiving person.

The following steps will help you to forgive because forgiving is a decision you must make even when you do not feel like doing it.

1. Acknowledge you were hurt, and don't pretend the hurt is not there. This would be living in denial.

2. Do not wait until you feel like forgiving. You cannot let feelings rule your life. Decide to forgive and then follow through with it. Pray for God's help to forgive.

3. Decide never again to bring up the offense with the offender. Do not dwell on the offense in your own mind. When it comes up, switch your thoughts to something else.

4. Do not discuss the offense with others or speak evil of the offender. If somebody brings it up or speaks against the offender, just say, "I prefer not to discuss it."

5. Do not expect to forget the offense. You cannot help but remember, but this does not mean you have not forgiven.

I heard about a man who murdered the only child of a family. The family wanted to show the murderer that they had forgiven him, so they asked the judge to excuse his sentence. They were confusing forgiveness with justice. Forgiving does not mean excusing an offense even if the offender has repented. We are to forgive by refusing to hate the person or dwelling on the offense. We then allow God and authorities to deal with that person as justice dictates. Also, forgiveness does not mean that we should return to an abusive situation. We can forgive without submitting to further abuse or endangerment.

Today's questions are essentially the same as they were yesterday, but from a different perspective.

Questions:

1. What unforgiving attitude have you had or is currently troubling you?

2. What keeps you from forgiving?

3. When will you be ready to do this?

4. Do you think you can do this on your own?

5. Can you trust God to handle all the consequences?

Day 6 – Chastisement
Read: Hebrews 12:5-11

I was playing in the front yard with my little son when he turned and ran into the street. I quickly overtook him, seized him by the arm, and pulled him back into the yard. I gave him several swats on the backside with my open hand and sternly told him, "No, no! Stay out of the street!"

My hand didn't hurt him as much as the disapproval and reprimand. He cried as though his heart had been broken. Fortunately, at that time in early 1960, I wasn't to be arrested for child abuse. But why did I do this? Did I dislike my son? Did I take pleasure in hurting him, or was I trying to protect him? Of course, we know it was the latter reason. I wanted to indelibly impress upon him that the street was dangerous territory for him at his level of maturity.

Through Moses, God gave the Israelites a system of dietary rules called Kosher. It has been found that many of those laws were based on good health practices. One well-known law was that pork was unclean and should not be eaten. We know now what only God knew then: that pork was infected with a parasite leading to deadly trichinosis. Another example of God's care is shown in the New Testament. The disciples were criticized for eating with unwashed hands. It was a "ceremonial" practice to wash before eating. This practice was handed down from God because He knew about germs long before they were discovered by science. God instituted these laws to His chosen people at a time when they were needed to protect them from unknown dangers. He continues to instruct us through the Holy Spirit to bring us into subjection because He knows what is best for us.

Some modern psychologists teach that we need to allow our children to learn from their own experiences and mistakes. The problem with this approach is that we don't always learn. Furthermore, the experience can be extremely harmful, causing severe injury, even death, before the lesson is learned. The guiding hand of a loving parent is necessary to protect us from experiences from which we may never recover. God is like that with us. As a caring father, He loves us too much to leave us the way we are. He knows what dangers lay ahead and wants to protect us from damaging experiences. He wants to see us grow into healthy, happy, mature men and women.

However, we don't always want to listen. We think we know better and God is just a big bully insisting on His own way and wants to ruin all our fun. When we rebel, we think we have a better way. The world tells us to "Go ahead if it feels good, do it." Just like Eve in the Garden of Eden, we don't believe anything bad is going to come from our actions. It won't happen to us. We think we know more than God does. How ludicrous! As you grow in Christ you will find more joy in pleasing Him than any fun you might ever have had in disobedience. And what is more, you will save yourself and your loved ones a ton of disorder and hurt. That is what maturity is all about, and we will learn more about it in Study 5, "Growing."

Questions:

1. Can you remember a time when something you thought was bad actually turned out good for you?

2. Have you rebelled against authority, and how did it work for you?

3. Do you look at the Christian life as being all about "Thou shalt not?"

4. Did either of your parents fail to guide you, and in what way?

5. Can you think of somebody whom you thought was mean, but now you see that they really helped you?

Day 7 – Pride of Life
Read: 1 John 1:9

God loves you. You are most precious in His sight. God's foremost desire is that you, as well as all creation, be redeemed. Because you were created in God's image you are already precious, but beyond that, you are pursued by God as a lover pursues the beloved. You matter to God. The One who is immeasurably worthy has declared you of worth to God.

Still, after being pursued and deemed worthy, we are not satisfied. Why is that? It might be because our culture teaches us not to be satisfied with the value that God has placed upon our lives. Our culture teaches us that our value comes from our productivity, our beauty, our fame, our money, or our skill. But our culture's lies aren't the root of this discontent. This problem is much older. This tendency to be dissatisfied with the value we have as God's beloved creation and to seek prestige and worth for ourselves is an ancient practice. It is the original sin. Adam and Eve desired to be more, more than God intended them to be. They were tricked into believing that they could do something to make themselves more important, more intelligent, and more worthy than merely the beloved creation of the Almighty God. Of course, they couldn't become more; they could only become less. We tend to believe the same lies they believed. But there is no improvement to be made from the status of the beloved creation of the Almighty God; that is as good as it gets!

There is a name for this human tendency: pride. Pride is the sin that comes from claiming that we are worthy apart from God, that our value is found in ourselves, our place in the world, and not in our creation. To say we are worthy is to worship ourselves. Pride is idolatry. It is the root of sin, and it is serious business. Pride blocks grace because our pride insists we don't need grace, so we turn from God and refuse it. If we are going to take grace seriously, we must take pride seriously. We must name it as a sin. We must fight the pride that grows in us. And to do that we must become people who confess.

Confession is a deceptively simple discipline. Confession is nothing more than honest speech to ourselves and to God (and sometimes to others) about who we are, what we have done, and what we believe. Confession is the discipline that defeats our tendency to look to ourselves as objects of worship, to look to our achievements and our skills, our beauty, and our human heritage for our value. We have a role in God's kingdom, no matter how weak we are. We can confess our weakness because God's grace has given us a place in the kingdom. We can confess our needs because God is able to meet them. We can confess our flaws and failures because God loves us no matter what. Consequently, as Matthew 18 tells us, we should expect to be loved by the church no matter how flawed and unfaithful we have been.

God's dream for His church is just this beautiful. There is no need to fear confession because we have built our community on grace. God wants to free us from our sins even more than we want to be free. God's one desire is to see us as a new creation. To begin the discipline of confession and begin the battle against the strong sin of pride, we must become proclaimers of grace. If a hundred times I have been told, "You did such a good job. You should be proud of yourself," then a thousand times I need to hear, "You matter because you are the Creator's beloved." If a hundred times I have been told, "You are worthless; you don't matter to anyone," then a thousand times I need to hear, "You matter because you are the Creator's beloved."

Questions:

1. How does it make you feel to know that God loves you even with all the bad things in your background?

2. How do you show pride in the way you live?

3. What keeps you from feeling satisfied with your life?

4. Think about the things you need to confess and pray to God that He will forgive you and help you to live in obedience to Him.

STUDY 3 – DECISIONS

Day 1 – Is God in Control?
Read: Deuteronomy 30:19-20; John 10:14-15

Decisions, decisions, decisions! Virtually every minute of the day, we are faced with making decisions. What time should I wake up? What shall I eat for breakfast? Will I go to work? How will I act when I am treated unfairly? Will I accept the invitation to a party where I know there will be drugs and alcohol? These are the deliberate and conscious decisions we must make. Unfortunately, we are often unprepared to make the right decisions. We will let the feelings of the moment affect good judgment rather than what we know to be right or wrong. That is why the first study of truth is so important: to know that we are not adrift in an uncertain world but have an absolute truth to follow. Knowing this makes decision-making so much easier and more certain. Ultimately, the decisions we make will affect the course of our lives because the person we are is the sum total of all the past decisions we have made.

Now is the time to change the course of your life. You can begin making decisions based on the Word of God. Now is the time to reject the leading of the flesh and begin abiding by the Spirit of God.

There are often two parts to every decision. The first part is purposing to make the right decision. That part is easy. But the "rubber meets the road" when we must follow through and act upon that decision. It is easy to say I will get up at 6:00 AM to be at work on time, but it is totally another thing when it comes time actually to do it. When your sleep is interrupted by the racket of the alarm, are you going to let that momentary feeling influence you to turn it off and roll over for those extra 40 winks? Will you excuse your wrong decision because you chose to stay up and watch the late show instead of going to bed on time? How many times have you done that and ended up late for work or a missed appointment? Eventually the consequences of repeated bad decisions will catch up to you. It may result in possible disciplinary action by your boss, a loss of your job, or even incarceration.

This is not the way God wants you to live. He said, *"I have come that they may have life and that they may have it more abundantly."* God wants your integrity, your "yes" to be yes, and your "no" to be no. He expects you to keep your word, to be consistent and committed in all your actions. When you make an appointment, you are expected to be on time. Your integrity, the kind of person you are is what is at stake! Other people will pass judgment on the God you profess by your integrity. If you fail to maintain your integrity, you will also fail in other areas of your life. You will try to put the blame on others, but eventually, you will realize it is from your own failures, and you will see your self-respect fade away. As it does, depression is the likely result. Unfortunately, some counselors will give you pills to relieve the depression instead of dealing with the factors that are responsible for it. One bad decision just leads to another.

Questions:

1. Name a bad decision that you have made that resulted in great trouble.

2. Did you know you were making the wrong choices at the time?

3. What caused you to make such a decision?

4. How do you think you would handle the same decision if you were faced with it again today?

5. Do you believe God will help you in making other tough decisions in the future?

Day 2 – First Choices
Read: Joshua 24:14-28

In the first two studies, we explored the subjects of Truth and Grace. Now, as we study decisions, it is time to make the most important decision of your life: whether you are willing to surrender your life to following Jesus. Until you have decided to follow Him, you are not prepared to make any other decisions in life. This is because, without the inner guidance of the Holy Spirit, you cannot know God's plan for you or be able to comprehend the Word of God fully.

You may have heard the expression, "Today is the first day in the rest of your life." This is because once you choose to live for Christ, you embark on a whole new way of thinking and living. Everything becomes new. As far as God is concerned, the old life is wiped away. Now, that doesn't mean you will forget it or that you won't have to live with the consequences of the past. It just means that everything is new in your relationships from this point on. The old life has passed away. Now is the time to commit yourself to a new way of life. You can begin living for Christ and not yourself. You see, it is not about you, it is not about me, it is not about others, it is about Him! Until you completely accept this idea, you will not find success in life or in your relationships.

When you choose to follow Him and give Him full control over your being, He will help you in making decisions. You will learn from His Word how to respond to the adverse circumstances that come your way. Most importantly, you can trust that He is in control. With Him, there are no chance circumstances. He is never surprised. As you grow in Him, you will discover that there is no longer what others call "coincidence." I know a person who had come to this understanding during participation in the Overcomers in Christ program held in a local detention center. He was facing a day in court in which he was hoping to receive a light sentence. He announced to the study group that whatever the outcome, whether he was to receive a light sentence or get the maximum of 25 years, it was in God's hands, and he would accept the outcome as coming from God. When he returned to class after sentencing, he announced that he was to serve 25 years without parole. He was praising God and tearfully hugging everybody in the group because he accepted the outcome from the hand of God. This powerful testimony had a dramatic impact on the entire institution, including the staff! While serving his sentence, he had to have heart bypass surgery, which he now says would have been the cause of his death had he not been incarcerated, where he received adequate medical care.

Why, then, do bad things happen to us after we surrender to Him and allow Him to control us? At times, when we are stressed by some difficult circumstance, it can be very hard to understand why He allows such things to afflict us. Dr. James Dobson explains this in his book "*Why Bad Things Happen to Good People.*" For now, we just have to trust Him. We can know for a certainty from His written Word that He knows our circumstances, that He loves us, and that He will see us through it all. He will even use these troubles to help develop us into the person He desires us to be.

God will not abandon us, so we must not abandon Him. Satan is the enemy. When you hear a voice saying in your mind that God cannot help or that He wouldn't allow this to happen if He really loved you, you can know that it is Satan who is planting those thoughts. Our separation from God and eventual destruction is Satan's single-minded goal. The conscious decisions you make have more influence on your life than all of the chance circumstances that intrude upon you over which you have no control. This is because God allows you to make decisions about how to respond to those chance circumstances. He often allows them as a test of your faith.

Questions:

1. Have you made the decision to follow Christ? If not, turn to Appendix I for instructions on how you can make the decision to receive Him as Lord of your Life.

2. What does following Christ mean to you?

3. What things do you think Jesus expects you to do since you have become a follower?

4. What decisions will you make right now to show that you have chosen to follow Jesus?

Day 3 – Commitment
Read: Philippians 3:12-14

In the military, I was taught that the mission was central to all our thoughts and actions. When sent out on patrol, we were not to allow ourselves to be distracted from getting the job done. We had to have a clear objective and be committed to carrying it out. If the bridge was out, you repelled into the chasm, swam across the raging waters, and climbed the rock wall on the other side. You didn't have the option to go back to camp and say, "The bridge was out, so we decided to come back."

In places, Scripture describes us as soldiers. In Ephesians 6:10-17 our battle armor is described in detail. In 2 Timothy 2:3, Paul describes us as soldiers engaged in warfare. He also equates our walk with competing in an athletic contest, saying we must obey the rules and "run the race" to win the prize. Our spirit is at war with the flesh. To overcome the desires of the flesh, we have to set our minds on the spirit. We have to make a conscious decision to turn away from the weakness of the flesh. Much of the time, we make bad decisions without considering the result. What will we say to our King Jesus when we fail in our assigned mission?

There is no commandment that says "Be Ye Committed." Commitment is not mentioned among the gifts of the Spirit, nor is it listed with the fruit of the Spirit in Galatians 5:22, yet the Bible is all about commitment. Commitment means that we "stay the course." We remain true to our decisions and refuse to be led astray. We must never lose sight of our goal of obedience to Christ by serving others and glorifying His Holy name. Anytime we waver from this goal, it is a sin. We must confess our wrongdoing and get right back to the task.

Our integrity as a child of God is dependent on keeping our commitments. If we think we will "try" to keep them, we are admitting that we might not succeed. We must say, "I will remain faithful" by **the power of God working in me**, and that power is made available by study and prayer. The unbelieving world is watching us, you, to see if you are for real. They want to know if you are real and whether this "religious stuff" really works. When you tell somebody you are going to meet them at a certain time and place, you are expected to be there and be on time! To not show up or to be late is a reflection of your own integrity. The same is true for being at work on time.

I was mentoring a man who was trying to get his life together. He got a new job as a mechanic, for which he was expected to have his own tools. He told his employer that he had to retrieve them from his former workplace. After scheduling my next meeting with him, I decided to collect some tools I didn't need or for which I had duplicates. I put them into a toolbox I wasn't using and was prepared to give them to him to fulfill his obligation. However, he didn't show up for the next meeting, and I didn't know where to find him. The next time I saw him, he no longer had the job. You see, he didn't show up for the blessing. It can be the same way with God when we fail to keep our commitments and be where He plans to bless us.

Questions:

1. What things stand in the way of your integrity?

2. Discuss this with your mentor and be accountable for your commitments.

3. Does it help you to see yourself as a soldier on a "mission?"

4. Will you commit to always being on time for meetings with your mentor and others?

Day 4 – Choosing Friends
Read: 1 Corinthians 15:33

As you begin your new life in Christ, you have to choose between healthy and damaging relationships. There is an old saying, "Birds of a feather flock together." This is true of human beings as well as birds. The people with which you choose to associate and those you call friends tell something about you. You choose to be around those with whom you are comfortable, those who share your values. If your friends curse, drink, fight, and tell course jokes then it is likely you do many of the same things. Otherwise, you would find their behavior offensive and withdraw from their company. This is explained by another old saying, "You are judged by the company you keep." When you turn from the old life to follow Jesus, you have become a new creature; you take on a new set of values. You have asked Him to come into your heart and transform your mind. How can this be true when you continue to associate with your former friends of the world?

An uncle of mine had terrible luck with women, or so it would seem. He had a stormy relationship before divorcing his first wife. He married again and began to start a family, but this marriage also broke up. He confided in my mother that he just couldn't find a good woman with which he could have a good relationship and loving family as he admired in others. My mother told him that he should allow her to pick a wife for him. You see, he was picking his wives from bar stools.

When Christ comes into our lives it requires us also to turn away from our old places and the friends that would lead us astray. We cannot help but be influenced by the company we keep, so we must be careful about choosing our friends. The places we go and our relationships have a powerful influence on our actions. I know of a young man who was out with his friends. The group accepted him because he had a car and a driver's license. He drove them to the home of a drug dealer, where they planned to get some drugs. The dealer was also a friend of the young man. But he didn't know that someone in the group was armed. When the transaction went bad, the dealer was shot and killed. The perpetrators returned to the car, and they sped away. The driver was later arrested, tried, and sentenced for his part in the murder. It wasn't anything he planned or wanted to be part of. Nevertheless, he suffered the consequences of the actions of his associates. What a tragedy as the result of poorly chosen friends.

Giving up our old friends isn't easy. We have attachments to them and they often try to continue the relationship. Being without them may make you feel vulnerable and lonely. They do not understand the changes that have taken place in you. Often, when you try to explain it, they will think you are putting them down. You must be careful not to pass judgment on them but to put the blame on yourself. Tell them that you have new interests and other things to do. Invite them to your Christian fellowship. However, they will not likely want to go because it is a place where they expect to feel uncomfortable.

Finding new friends is another challenge. It takes time to establish new friends and associates, but you will find that those in your church and fellowship share a common interest in serving the Lord Jesus. Be sure to look in the right places and reach out to others rather than waiting for them to come to you.

Questions:

1. List some names of old friends that you will have to avoid in your new life with Christ.

2. What former places will you have to avoid?

3. Where will you look for new friends?

4. What qualities will you look for in your new friend?

5. What qualities will you need to have so that others will want to be your friend?

Day 5 – Planning Ahead
Read: 1 Timothy 6:7-12

In *Aircraft Owners and Pilots Association* magazine, they run a feature called "Never Again." Each one tells about an event that happened to an airplane pilot that he proclaims will never happen again. As a pilot, I am often asked about the plane crash of John Kennedy, Jr. One person asked if such a thing could happen to me. Not knowing for sure what happened, it is difficult to say, but if my analysis is correct, it would not. Apparently, Kennedy was flying by visual reference during a time of poor visibility. Chances are a false horizon disoriented him. This means what he thought was the ground was, in reality, some lights, stars, or clouds that were at an angle. As he banked the plane to maintain what he thought was level flight, the airplane went into a dive. His Piper Saratoga would have accelerated so quickly that it would have been impossible to recover control from his altitude before hitting the water. I tried it on a flight simulator.

I am surprised with his training and aircraft equipment that such a thing would have happened. If I had been the pilot, I would have used the autopilot (Kennedy had one but wasn't using it) to control and guide the aircraft until over the airport at Martha's Vineyard. Once I had the airport in site I would have circled to land, so I don't think I would have made the same mistake Mr. Kennedy made.

"If I was in his shoes I would…" "There is no way I would do something like that." It seems that we have made up our minds to do certain things in certain situations or things we would not do. Of course, we do not always know how we might act when actually confronted with a given situation. However, it is good to have already considered what actions we may or may not take. Often, a plan of action is set in our minds. This is how we must learn to walk on our spiritual journey. It is especially true if you have been a slave to activities such as using drugs or abusing alcohol. You have to plan ahead so you are prepared to handle temptations and head off anticipated problems.

What do you do or say if someone offers you your previous substance of abuse, whether it is legal alcohol or illegal drugs? What will you say? Have you thought about this? Do you know what reason you will give? Such decisions need to be made now, not when the opportunity confronts you. Very often you will be faced with making a decision in a weakened condition. This is dangerous, so you have to decide now and not feel embarrassed when the time comes. The offer of alcohol could come from one of your new Christian friends who is unaware that you were once enslaved by it. You can say, "I have learned that I can't control my drinking, so I have decided to avoid it altogether."

What if an old friend invites you to a party where you know there will be temptations? How can you say "no" without offending the person? You probably can't, but you can be gracious if you have rehearsed your answer. A rehearsed answer will make the words come easier and avoid telling a lie in order to turn the person down. You may be tempted to make an excuse like "I am busy" when you are not. So, you say, "I have decided not to party anymore because I know what trouble it has caused in the past."

What if you are tempted by sex? Where will you attend worship or will you stay home this Sunday because you want to sleep in or have other things to do? Should I go to work this morning after being out late the previous evening? All of these, and many more decisions, have to be made on a regular basis, and not all the answers can be given to you. You have to think ahead and make plans for how you will respond to each situation. For example, when you decide to stay out late you should be thinking about how it will be difficult to get up and go to work on time. This is all a part of being a consistent, mature child of God, bringing honor to Him, and keeping your own life in order.

Questions:

1. Can you think of times when you got into trouble because you chose to be in the wrong place?

2. What activities will you need to avoid in order to maintain your new life in Jesus?

3. Make a plan with your mentor as to how you will handle future temptations.

Day 6 – What is the Cost of Following Jesus?
Read: Luke 18:19-27

This Scripture reading may cause you to wonder if you are able to follow Jesus. Does God really expect you to sell everything and give the money away before you can be His follower? Just looking around at others who call themselves Christians may cause you to wonder, "What did Jesus mean by this statement?" Jesus knows our hearts. He knew that this rich young ruler was enslaved by his possessions. So, Jesus challenged him to make a decision about his heart and his values. Sadly, the man valued his possessions more than he valued his desire for God.

You may have wondered why people give to the church or how much should be given. Maybe you have heard about tithes and offerings and wondered what that means. Very many people have no understanding as to how the church uses the money that is received. That is no excuse for not giving, but it is a challenge to learn more about church finances. Like the rich young ruler, people have turned away from the church because of differences over money. I met a new Christian who insisted that his money belonged to him and neither God nor the church had anything to say about what he did with it. While nobody has the right to judge you regarding your money, your giving reveals the attitude of your heart. You should be a tougher judge of yourself than others are.

In a later study, we will look at the many different ways to give of ourselves, but for now, we will look at how God expects us to manage the money He has given to us. This is called stewardship and is foundational to our later understanding of giving. Jesus had a lot to say about our money. That is because He understands how we are made. He knows what motivates us. He said in Matthew 6:21,

"Wherever your treasure is, there your heart will be also."

Jesus expects us to use the money we earn to provide for our earthly needs, but He also wants us to place money in proper

55

perspective and to be good stewards of it. As a believer and servant of Christ we must come to the realization that everything we have comes to us from God. He provides us with bodily strength, a healthy mind, and a set of skills with which we can earn money. In James 1:17, we are told,

"Every good and every perfect gift is from above, and comes down from the Father of lights…"

God is the "Potentate," the one who exercises absolute power over all things. As our Lord, the giver and sustainer of life, He is entitled to it all. But He isn't a demanding God. Because of His love and grace, because He has also allowed us the freedom to act on our own, He allows us to decide how we will manage what He has provided. Concerning the "collection for the saints," Paul tells the Corinthians, "On the first day of the week, they should put aside a portion of the money they have earned." The first day means we are to give to God first and trust Him to meet our other needs. Trust is what gives meaning to our relationship with Him. Part of that trust is to meet our financial commitments. As servants of the Most High we make it a priority to pay our obligations and to pay them on schedule. Failure to set priorities and meet our obligations reflects poorly on the fellowship of believers and on our Lord.

It has been the custom of the Christian church (believers) to give 10% at the beginning of the week. The term "tithe" means a tenth part. In Deuteronomy 14:23 it says, "Tithing teaches us to fear God." This is a valuable lesson in learning to give. We give the "first fruits" of our labor and don't wait until the end of the week to see how much is left over for our giving to the Lord. When we give the first part to God, we trust Him to supply the remainder of our needs. This is a test of faith. If we are faithful in our giving, we are trusting God to supply the rest of our needs. J.C. Penney tried to out-give God. He gave 80% of his income to the work of the Lord, but God kept giving him more. He said he never could outgive the Lord.

Rather than being greedy and gathering as much as you can, God wants you to exercise wisdom and good judgment about handling money. In Luke 14:28-30, He says it would be foolish to start building a tower before counting the cost. This implies that you should plan how to handle money. A budget is a tool to help you to handle money. Giving the first 10% to the Lord and the next 10% to yourself is a good place to start in creating a budget. This means you save money for emergencies, major expenditures, and income during times of unemployment, so you will not be a burden to others. The remaining 80% is then appropriated for paying bills. We are not like the government; when we do not have enough, it means we have to look for ways to cut spending. Living this way actually leads to financial freedom because we control our money and will not let it control us.

Questions:

1. What happens when you try to justify exceptions for giving less than a tithe to God?

2. List some things you think you need that are more important than giving to God.

3. Does living on a budget sound threatening to you? In what ways might a budget give you more freedom?

4. What debts or obligations do you have right now that need to be taken care of?

Day 7 – Applying Wisdom
Read: Romans 12:17-21

When I was a teenager, I was obsessed with striking back at anyone who offended me. I would be completely absorbed in finding ways to strike back. I wanted to hurt them for what they did to me. Over time, God has helped me escape from this snare of the devil. I remember a time, much later in life, when I was working with a person with whom I had a very strained relationship. We did not agree with each other, probably because we were competing for the favor of our demanding boss. One evening, before my eyes closed for sleep, I prayed that Jesus would change my attitude toward this person and that He would help me care for her in a way that would glorify Him. As I was praying, a warm feeling came over my body. It sort of tingled like a warm shower of water being poured over me. I felt the animosity float away like a pressure being released from my body. I could tell without a doubt my prayer had been answered. The stressfulness of my thoughts toward her was replaced with pleasant feelings. I was transformed!

Shortly after that miracle of God's power, I was walking past the demanding boss's office, where I overheard her giving a false report, blaming me for one of her own misdeeds. I abruptly stopped in my tracks. I was about to turn around, walk into the office, and set the record straight. Before I could react, it *came upon me* (God's way of speaking) that I didn't have to do anything. Like everything in life, this situation was in God's hands. She couldn't hurt me unless God permitted it. I moved on my way without further concern. I later learned that the boss knew the truth, and the incident raised my status with the boss. Too often, we fail to make a decision by reacting to circumstances.

When others hurt us, we immediately strike back without thinking. Perhaps you have come from a background that has taught you to hurt those who hurt you. This is not God's way. He wants you to apply forethought to your relationships. You must learn that reaction is not always necessary and most often results in bad behavior, leading to unintended consequences. First, you have to stop and think. It is better to do nothing than do the wrong thing. Then, you must be big enough and strong enough to take the hurt without attempting to even the score. You have to trust God with every aspect of your life. You need to discern whether or not a response is necessary and then learn how to do this in a way that honors God and does not hurt others. Failing to live this way will allow the actions of others to make your decisions for you. Why should you let your mistakes allow the ones who hurt you to continue inflicting damage? Let God's instruction from the Bible determine the way you live, not the words or actions of your enemies.

We live in a world that seeks and values immediate gratification. We are not willing to work and wait until we can have things we think we need. I illustrate this in the following way. If I offer you one million dollars right now or 1 penny today, the amount doubled each day for 30 days, which would you choose? The answer appears obvious, but of course, you are expecting a trick question, so you hesitate to answer. Like most people, you probably would choose the one million dollars. If you did, you short-changed yourself by $4,368,709. Do the math! That is the result of immediate gratification instead of thinking things through and being willing to wait for the good things to come.

In listening to Dr. Laura Schlessinger on the radio, I often hear callers say they already knew what answer she would give them, but they just wanted her confirmation. Most people know in their mind the right decision to make but it is often hard to go against our emotions. We must be willing to take our concerns, problems, temptations, and decisions to God. Share your burden with a trusted counselor. Make a list of pros and cons regarding the outcome of the decision until you are happy with either outcome. Pray before making decisions. In submitting them to God, you agree to surrender your desires to His will. This process has to be repeated until it becomes a habitual practice.

Questions:

1. Write about a time that you were angry and struck back at someone only to have your actions backfire. Discuss this with your mentor.

2. When have you failed to make a decision only to wish you had?

3. Have you ever struck back at someone only to regret it later?

4. What are you going to do in making a major decision that faces you right now?

5. Are you willing to commit it to God and accept the outcome either way?

STUDY 4 - CONNECT

Day 1 - Community

Read: John 12:24-26

"Very truly I tell you, unless a kernel of wheat falls to the ground and dies, it remains only a single seed. But if it dies, it produces many seeds. Those who love his life will lose it, while the one who hates life in this world will keep it for eternal life. Whoever serves me must follow me; and where I am, my servant also will be. My Father will honor the one who serves me."

Walking on the strong legs of grace and truth, we now turn to the path before us. Every step of this path has been walked by Jesus so we can go forth with confidence. We also know that His path led to a cross, so we go forth with some fear and trembling. Perhaps the greatest irony of Christian discipleship is that the life of a disciple is, at the same time, both free and costly. This new life is a gift. We are given the opportunity to turn from death to life. Our guide, Jesus, promises to watch our every step so that we do not stumble. Remember, our guide leads us up a mountain! At each step, Jesus calls us to climb out of the valley of the shadow of death that clings to us and climb toward the mountaintop. Each of these steps will require us to die a bit more to who we were and to whom the world wants us to be. As we go forward, we will look at five habits that marked Christ's walk on the earth: Connecting, Growing, Reaching, Giving, and Serving.

As you walk, you can be assured of two things: you will stumble, and you will wonder if these steps really matter. This is why you can only follow the way of Jesus on the legs of grace and truth. Grace has already forgiven you when you fall, and grace offers the real power for you to keep walking. Truth assures us that the Bible is a reliable guide and Christ is a true leader. Christ Himself is truth. No matter how different this way is from the ways the world has taught us, we can know that only this way leads to rest, only this way leads to abundant life, and only this way leads to the restoration of your life to what God has always intended.

Our next step in following Jesus is connecting. This is the practice of creating a community. As we have already seen, God's one purpose is to restore our relationships with Him and with one another. God does not have a list of individuals He wants to save; God wants to build a people, a nation, and a family. We participate in this endeavor when we practice the habit of connecting. Jesus developed intimate relationships with small groups of people who could know Him and be fully known by Him. These circles of relationship created a context in which Christ could be honest with those close to Him. He did not "get real" with everybody. In the same way, as we practice the habit of connecting, we must be intentional in our efforts to build honest and significant relationships with a close group of fellow followers. Likewise, we practice the discipline of connecting when we work to maintain the unity of the church, which is Christ's Body. Paul tells us that by God's Spirit, the church is one, but that reality is seldom achieved.

Connecting takes effort; striving for unity is hard work. As Paul writes to the Corinthians and the Romans, in a human body, no one part would ever say to another, "You are not needed." In the same way we must express our unity by our faithfulness to the whole body. Thirdly, we practice connecting by caring about the needs of others. The individualism of our culture is so strong that to us, it is almost inconceivable to put someone else's needs before our own. Yet this is precisely what is expected of us. This is what Christ has done for us and for all people, and to walk in His footprints is to do the same.

"But you are a chosen people, a royal priesthood, a holy nation, God's special possession, that you may declare the praises of him who called you out of darkness into his wonderful light. Once you were not a people, but now you are the people of God; once you had not received mercy, but now you have received mercy." 1 Peter 2:9-10

Questions:

1. How important do you think the local church is to what God and Jesus are trying to accomplish?

2. How has the church hurt God's mission over the years?

3. How has the mission of Christ been affected by our failure to live in harmony with each other?

4. What specific practice of connecting could you begin to follow?

Day 2 – Reconciliation
Read: Read John 17:20–26

Jesus is praying for us. What is His prayer? Bask a moment in the glorious and humbling irony that in this one instance, we can, by our choices and by the power of God's grace, contribute to answering the prayer of Jesus. Amazing!

The studies of *Free at Last* are the principles of how to live the abundant life of a Christ follower. They flow from two interwoven questions: What are the crucial character traits of God, and what are the crucial character traits for people who want to follow God? In every case, these studies express the truth about the nature and heart of God. These do not just act to which God has called us, although that would be enough. These are also values and actions that God demonstrates. God is committed to connecting. God's deep desire is to build a relationship with each of us. He longs to see us in healthy relationships with each other. At the end of the day, God's one purpose is a connecting purpose. A look through Scripture shows us a God who has never wavered in pursuing these connections.

In the time of the prophet Jeremiah, God's people seemed to do everything they could to destroy the relationship they had with God. Jeremiah's predecessor, a prophet named Isaiah, warned that the connection with God was so seriously ruptured that unless they turned back to Him, they would be destroyed. In this desperate, broken relationship, God had every right to walk away or turn His anger against them. Instead, God comes toward them to restore what they had broken. Again and again, God tells of a coming day when all relationships will be restored. God says through Jeremiah,

> *"My eyes will watch over them for their good, and I will bring them back to this land. I will build them up and not tear them down...I will give them a heart to know me, that I am the LORD. They will be my people, and I will be their God, for they will return to me with all their heart." Jeremiah 24:6,7*

Through the darkest times, God is looking to restore relationships. Even when we disappoint and deny Him, God pursues us. God is committed to connecting! Connecting is not just a small part of God's character. It's at the very core of who God is. God is, by nature, relational. God is described in Scripture as Father, Son, and Spirit, three, and yet one in the most intimate of relationships with each other. It's a great mystery where Father and Son are described as one (John 10:30), where the Holy Spirit is God's Spirit, a part of God and yet also somehow distinct.

God's own nature is a picture of connecting in the deepest of ways. The word often used to describe this relationship is "trinity," yet the reality is that no word or explanation can adequately capture the depth of this divine connection. It's an amazing mystery that within God, the Father, Son, and Spirit are connected in relationship. And here's something even more amazing: this God of relationships invites us into this intimate circle of fellowship. What God longs for is to see us re-connected with one another and with God in ways that mirror this deep, powerful divine connection we see within the Trinity.

Questions:

1. In Jesus' prayer for us (John 17:20–26), He prays that we would enjoy the same kind of unity that He has with God. Single words like fellowship or community are only the "tip of the iceberg" for what this would look like. What actions would that kind of community relationship require from us?

2. How does knowing God's desire and nature about connecting change your thoughts about what it means to follow Christ?

3. Why do you think people claim that their faith is a private matter between them and God?

4. How much time and what behaviors would help us connect with God? Can we do it in an hour and a half on Sunday mornings? Can we do it alone?

5. Do the people in your circle of friends know that God's deepest desire is for us to be in a relationship with God and with one another? What can you do to make them aware of God?

Day 3 - Fellowship
Read: 1 Corinthians 12:12-27

In the same way that God's nature is characterized by connecting, God calls believers to connect to each other in the deepest of ways. This special connected harmony is described with a powerful metaphor in the New Testament. We as individuals are connected together making up the Church, the Body of Christ. This is a special connection, that while remaining independent, we are nevertheless harmoniously functioning together as a living organism. Looking at the way body parts are connected helps us see how we are to function as parts of Christ's Body.

The Bible also makes it clear that maintaining unity takes effort on our part. All of us who make up Christ's Body have to work together to maintain unity. This may require us to swallow pride or even endure wrongdoing. It takes a positive attitude and special effort to achieve unity. It takes a spirit of love and caring for each other. Sometimes, churches or groups of Christians experience divisiveness because they stubbornly focus on those issues that divide rather than those that unite us.

Each of us has one body. If I lop off my index finger while dicing carrots, it doesn't become a separate body. If it's not surgically reattached in the right way, it dies! In the same way, the Bible teaches that God's people are one people. Sometimes, Christians make the mistake of cutting themselves off from others who are following Christ. I have often heard the phrase, "You don't have to go to church to be a Christian." While this may be true in general principle, it is not what we would call "best practices." When we do this, we cannot fully live. Failing to connect with Christ's church or avoiding connection with others connected to Jesus cuts us off from the one body God intends for us.

Let's say you accidentally put your hand on a hot stove. Immediately, the flesh on your palm begins to burn. What happens? In a microsecond, your nerves flash a 911 signal to the muscles in your arm and body. Suppose your muscles form a subcommittee on the issue of burning flesh and call a meeting. The agenda is set, minutes are taken, and they deliberate questions: Do we have the resources to deal with the skin's problem? What is the root cause of the skin's problem? Who authorized the hand to touch the hot stove? What should we do to prevent this in the future? Do we really care about this problem?

Isn't that silly? Real bodies react very differently, don't they? In real life, the rest of your body would immediately leap into action—including a yelp (hopefully nothing worse) from your tongue—and a muscle reaction to move your burning hand away from the heat source. That's how it is in the body of Christ. Paul teaches that when any part of the body is hurt or suffering, the whole body should react to ease the pain.

Mike and Sue were devastated to learn their pregnancy would miscarry. It seemed like the world was caving in on them. They wanted to hide in their pain, pulling away from the church. But as they shared their sorrow with fellow believers, they found themselves surrounded, loved, and prayed for through their sadness. They learned how important it is to be part of a body, where the parts know naturally to help and care for each other. Every one of us will experience pain and difficulty in our lives, but we are not meant to go through it alone. The church is where deep connections allow us to help each other at life's hardest and harshest moments. The way Paul says it,

"If one part suffers, every part suffers with it; if one part is honored, every part rejoices with it." 1 Corinthians 12:1-26.

Some organizations created by men have different levels of membership. But when we join ourselves in the Body of Christ, every part has the same "full" membership status. None are considered greater or lesser than the others. Each part is dependent on the function of others. Parts that are vulnerable or weak have higher protection. Our internal organs are guarded by our chest muscles and ribcage. Parts that are attractive and impressive are no longer important. In fact, it is easier for me to live without an eye or a hand than without a liver!

The Bible tells us we are in the world, but we must not be of the world. We are told not to be unequally yoked with unbelievers. While we are called to be joined together into the body of Christ, we must also separate ourselves from unhealthy relationships. This doesn't mean that we are to be rude or hateful, but we need to be careful with whom we develop relationships. Our friends must be those who care about our spiritual welfare and who will not lead us away from our Christian community.

Questions:

1. Which statements about the Body of Christ are you most ready to embrace? Which is a struggle for you to accept?

2. What actions can you take to become more sensitive to pain in the whole Body of Christ?

3. How is your mission for Christ affected when you are separated from other believers?

4. How can you be a support to those parts of the body that are "weaker?"

Day 4 – Hospitable
Read: Genesis 18:1-8

When I arrived at summer camp for the ROTC officer's training, I found my bunk and put my things away. I then began greeting other men as they came into the barrack and helped them find their place and stow their gear. My actions didn't go unnoticed by the leaders, and I had the highest rating in the platoon during that first week. This is what hospitality and service is all about. We are to be like Jesus, seeking out those on the outside, welcoming them, and inviting them in. Simply put, hospitality is the art of making people feel "at home." When a church lacks hospitality, it is missing something central to Jesus' message and will die. But a church that practices hospitality will thrive.

Let's look at another example of hospitality from the book of Acts 11:19–30. The city of Antioch was a massive trade center. It was the third largest city in the Roman Empire and had perhaps the most diverse population. Antioch's residents spoke dozens of languages and came from many ethnic groups. Into this city, early Christians came to share the Gospel soon after the church began. At first, they followed the custom of sharing the Gospel only with the Jews, but soon, they began to share with all people. As a result, many came to Christ. The church had many gifted leaders and grew dramatically. What was so impressive about the Antioch church was its hospitality. For the first time Jews and Gentiles were connecting with each other in sharing and fellowship. A most peculiar thing was happening: these Christian Jews and Christian Gentiles were eating together! This was a radical, new thing since Jewish law forbids such table fellowship with non-Jews. But these Christ followers knew that Christian love demands exactly this kind of table fellowship. Hospitality isn't just a harmless hobby for homemakers who know how to put out towels and run a Bed and Breakfast. Sometimes it's gutsy and gritty. In a radical act of devotion to Christ that clashed with long-standing tradition, the Christians of the Antioch church opened their homes to let anyone come to the table. They knew that in Christ, all races, nations, and people were one and that sharing a meal around a common table was a mark of unity.

That's a picture of hospitality. But then came trouble (Galatians 2:1–13). Peter visited and participated in this unique fellowship. With every bite, he demonstrated what he had learned from Christ: God shows no favoritism. But then a group from Jerusalem showed up and said that even after accepting Christ, Jews should still maintain ritual purity, and that meant not participating in table fellowship with Gentile Christians. Peter knew what was true, but he didn't stand up for it. He had tasted Christ-like hospitality, but now he and the other Jewish Christians stopped eating and connecting with the Gentile Christians. When Paul saw this, he publicly confronted Peter. Paul knew that there was a lot at stake in this "hospitality issue." It could split the church because the church is a web of relationships, and hospitality creates and strengthens those relationships. The Antioch church was built on the practice of hospitality in a pagan world. The threat to that practice would have crippled their mission, at the least, and most likely would have destroyed the Antioch church.

Hospitality is equally essential to the life of the church today. Hospitality parks are further from the church building, so first-time guests can have the closest parking spaces. Hospitality seeks out the newcomer who looks a little lost before worship service instead of chatting with long-time friends. Hospitality makes room in your home, makes room in your group, and makes room at your dinner table. Hospitality makes room in your life - in your heart - for those Jesus wants to draw into connection with Him graciously.

Questions:

1. Can you relate to a time when you were shown hospitality?

2. Can you relate to a time when you were denied hospitality?

3. How did it make you feel?

4. Can you describe the difference between being kind and being hospitable?

5. How can you begin to show hospitality to others?

Day 5 – Being Real
Read: Matthew 23:25-29

Maybe you have grown up being the "tough guy," hiding behind a mask that protects you or prevents you from being real to the people around you. Maybe you have erected walls to prevent exposing any weaknesses, especially if you are a new baby Christian in a situation where you perceive strength as a protective necessity. In order for you to become real and to be transparent to others, you need the courage to remove that mask and show the real person that Christ wants you to be.

Anyone who has been incarcerated knows that when you are closely confined with others, you can't hide anything from anyone. It's truer in prison than on the outside. You may be able to keep things from people a little longer on the outside than on the inside, but since everybody is closely packed together in prison, there is no privacy. Anything you do or say on the inside usually gets found out, so you can't really be a "closet Christian," and you definitely can't be a "closet tough guy." You can't be a tough guy in the dormitory, then go to church service or Bible study and come back and try to play tough guy all over again.

Everyone will see your hypocrisy.

You hear people talk about hypocrites or "jail-house" religion. Trying to maintain the dual standards of Transparent Christian and Tough Guy is where the hypocrisy accusation originates. The truth is, God knows your heart, and so do you, but it isn't easy to be transparent because this requires letting your guard down. As soon as you do, those around you will expect to see changes in your attitude and actions. They will be quick to point out inconsistencies in the way you live. You may want to obey God and follow Him, but you are afraid it may show weakness that others will take advantage of.

When you begin taking steps to become obedient to God, you will still have many bad habits and attitudes. This mixture of the old worldly man and the new spiritual one is not going to set well with others. Unlike God, they expect your whole life to change instantly, and it won't be long before you hear that dreaded accusation of "hypocrite." Immediately, the tough guy in you comes out, and you further prove their point. The tough guy attitude just digs you into a deeper hole.

Now is the time to try living God's way. Hiding behind that mask may seem like a safe way to live, but it only hinders you from becoming the person God wants you to be. You cannot grow closer to Him until you are ready to take off the mask and step into the truth.

"This is the message that we have heard from him and declare to you, that God is light and in Him there is no darkness at all. If we claim to have fellowship with Him, and walk in darkness, we lie and do not practice the truth." 1 John 1:5-6

Now, I am not suggesting that you call for everybody's attention and make a grand announcement, "Hey everybody, I just turned my life over to God, and I am not going to be like the rest of you anymore." This is going to offend others and cause trouble. However, you can start by privately sharing your newly found faith with others who may be sympathetic to you. Your attitude toward them should begin to change. You should see that they are people with needs, and you might lead them to help. The more you can learn about Scripture, the more opportunity you will find to share it with those in need. You can begin praying for those around you, even those in authority over you! God will hear your prayers.

His Word says, "The effectual and fervent prayer of a righteous man accomplishes much" (my emphasis added).

Maybe you can change your behavior toward the little guy you used to pick on and demonstrate to him how God is changing your life. In all, you can begin drawing closer to God and develop meaningful relationships with those around you, not by preaching at them or judging them, but by being kind, caring, and honest. Living for Christ isn't going to be easy, especially if you are in jail or prison, but He didn't call you to the easy life. You were called to be obedient, even when it isn't comfortable. You are called to begin living a new life that is centered on Him and that you will take with you wherever you go.

Questions:

1. What happens when two tough guys meet each other?

2. How much do you think God is impressed by the "Tough Guy" attitude?

3. What keeps you from letting your guard down and being kind to other people?

4. What kind of person do others truly care about and admire, the truly honest or the fake?

5. What holds you back from being honest and real?

Day 6 - Connecting Means Caring
Read: Philippians 2:1–4

When a baby is born, its life and energy are centered around very few things: "I'm hungry, I'm tired, I'm happy, I'm cranky. Feed me, let me sleep, change my diaper." We don't consider it selfish for an infant to be consumed with his or her own needs and desires. But as we grow up, hopefully, this changes. The Scriptures explain that following Christ will reverse the direction of our focus from inward to outward. As always, the example and motivation is Jesus.

"Each of you should look not only to your own interests but also to the interests of others."

Those words from Philippians 2:1- 4 present one of the most daunting challenges in the whole Bible. Here's how it is possible. As we think about people the same way Jesus thought about people, it changes our focus. It changes relationships. It gets my attention and energy from "me" and opens my eyes to how God can use me to bless and serve those around me.

When we think about others the way Jesus thinks about them, we will find ourselves actively caring about them. Think about the way Jesus cared about people. His compassion for large crowds and individual people moved him to heal the sick and hurting, feed the hungry, and comfort the harassed (Matthew 9:36; Matthew 14:14; Mark 8:2). Jesus wept with those who grieved and celebrated with those who rejoiced (John 2:1–11; John 11:33–36). Our Christ-like care for others should show in every aspect of our daily interaction. We may not perform miraculous healings, but we probably know someone who is sick or someone in a nearby hospital or nursing home we could comfort with our visit. We may not miraculously feed thousands, but surely there is someone who could use some groceries or a homeless shelter that needs volunteers to make sandwiches. Caring is not always about heroic efforts. It's mostly about our heart. Caring is having the heart of Jesus alive in us.

The early Christians were a tight-knit community that generously took care of their own. They were so genuinely connected to each other that they no longer thought of their possessions as "mine" or "yours" but rather "ours." Their sharing was so Christ-like that for a time, there were no needy among them (Acts 4:32–35). Eventually, the early Christians needed reminders to realign their attitude with that of Jesus. James warns that the Christ follower who sees their brother or sister needing clothes and food and does nothing has a faith that is dead (James 2:14–17). Christ gave away all He had for those He loved, including His own life. Following Him means sharing our time, our toys, our resources, and our very lives with others. When the heart of Jesus is alive in us, we will share. In one sense, Christ-like care is easy. We simply open our eyes to the needs all around us, needs in our church, our neighborhoods, and our community. Then, do something about it. That might mean starting small with one hour of caring or one person for whom to care. But if we're honest, we know that Christ-like care is hard. It's easier to act like the self-centered child.

Philippians 2:7–8 tells us that Jesus cared enough to die on the cross. Paul is not telling us we have to be martyred on the cross in order to follow Jesus. But he is challenging us to go far outside our comfort zone, because that's where the people are who need our care. None of us, not even Christians, escape from the hurts and troubles of real life. The beauty of it is that Christians can look to the support of those who accompany them on the walk. Paul makes a passing reference to the wrongful death sentence he faces, but he counts on the Philippians to support him by rejoicing with him (Philippians 2:17–18).

Today, Christians still suffer hard times, but Christians also still show loving care. Parents lose their newborn to a tragic illness, but their small group helps with little things like a meal and big things like tearful prayer. A church family suffers as a result of infidelity among some members, but loving student ministry volunteers circle the adolescent daughter with support and care. When natural or man-made disasters strike, invariably, churches and individuals are among the first to step forward to help relieve suffering without regard to faith or race.

We care and share because we walk in the footsteps of the One who cared enough to leave heaven and freely give His life away for us. We bear one another's sins by encouraging those who are overcome by temptation. We meet each other's financial and material needs. We weep and rejoice; we hurt and joyfully sing with one another. We are connecting the best when we are caring and sharing the most.

Questions:

1. How can you care about others like Jesus did?

2. Think about your actions and attitudes. Do you act like a self-centered child or a caring, giving, mature adult? Discuss this with your Mentor.

3. How is humility different from self-loathing and guilt?

4. Christ made your best interest a higher priority than His own. How does Christ's example shape the ways that you consider the interests of others?

5. How do we cultivate the kind of humility that Paul talks about?

Day 7 - The Church Divided
Read: I Corinthians 12:4-31

The story begins in a beautiful East Tennessee Valley. The little church in this valley became embroiled in a controversy. Many insisted that the coal bin should remain outside the building where it had stood since the initial construction. This kept the church clean and was how it had always been done. Others were sure that there was space for a furnace room in the little church, and the coal bin could then be moved inside. On cold winter days, this would make it easier for those charged with maintaining the fire. The debate over this issue grew fierce, and relationships were torn. Eventually, old, long forgotten grievances were remembered, and the church began to tear apart. Ultimately, the church split and half moved up the creek to worship in a different building. Of course, today, both buildings are heated and cooled by a heat pump. Although it was told to me as a fact, this may not be the way it really happened. Nevertheless, this is typical of many church splits.

The world has criticized the Christian church for its many divisions. They are confused and do not believe that any denomination has all the right answers. This comes about because we often focus on those things that divide us rather than those truths we hold in common. To make matters worse, we fuss and quarrel with each other over those differences. Many Christians refuse to attend the worship service of a different denomination. This is not what Christ wanted. Christ wanted His people to show love and acceptance of one another despite those differences.

In the decades following the American Revolution, a number of men and women caught this vision of Christian unity. They realized the amazing truth that by unifying their different churches and denominations, they could answer Jesus' prayer. The movement's leaders sought unity among all followers of Christ on the basis of common Bible truths on which all Christians could agree. They sought to follow the ancient Christian motto, "In essentials unity, in non-essentials liberty, and in all things love." Believers from dozens of denominations decided to drop their denominational labels and claim to be Christians only. Even more rare, they recognized that even those who kept denominational labels were part of the Christian community. Another motto reminded them, "We are not the only Christians, but we are Christians only." This movement called itself the Restoration Movement because it believed that through the appeal to Scripture and commitment to unity, the one church that Christ prayed for could be restored.

This movement has struggled along the way. In its own history it has divided over some of the same kind of things that divided the established denominations. But today, as I survey the church throughout the world, I am encouraged. All sorts of churches are coming together. Many people and many movements and denominations are recognizing that what we have in common is greater than what keeps us apart.

Christians with many different labels are working together to feed the hungry, house the homeless, and reach the lost through organizations like Feed the Hungry, World Vision, and Habitat for Humanity. United under the Lordship of Christ, Christian groups are beginning to work together instead of dividing.

You have a role in this great wind of change that is sweeping through the church. You can participate in answering the prayer of Jesus. Your role starts inside you. Refuse to participate in the division over non-essentials. Practice reconciliation and peacemaking. Do not be afraid to discuss differences, but look for issues where you can find common ground. Serve together, eat together, worship, and study in ways that overcome our self-imposed labels. If you align your heart and actions with Jesus' heart for unity, the Spirit will bless you with opportunities to connect. We will study this further in a later lesson on unity.

Questions:

1. Were you raised to believe in just one particular denomination?

2. In what ways have you found the differences in denominations confusing?

3. What are a few "essentials" that cannot be compromised?

4. What would you consider non-essential?

5. Do you think unity means all have to have the same label? Why or why not?

STUDY 5 – GROW

Day 1 - Change
Read: 1 Corinthians 3:6–7

God alone grows us. Acting as an agent of growth is an integral part of God's character. Like the sun that does not change but changes all that it touches, God is a growth agent of unparalleled power and beauty to all of His creation. As you read in the Gospel of Mark, God parallels spiritual growth with plant growth. Later, the apostle Paul describes the spiritual growth of the Corinthians:

> *"I planted, and Apollos watered, but God has been making it grow. So neither the one who plants nor the one who waters is anything, but only God who makes things grow."*

Encountering God will always leave people changed. In the same way that a seed buried in the earth flourishes under God's provision, we, too, will grow abundantly as we interact directly with God. God intends to bring re-creation to all things; if we will simply abide in Him. God knows our flaws, our weaknesses, and our immaturity and is ready to nurture and develop us.

It is not possible to encounter God in a personal relationship and remain unchanged. There are some beautiful examples of characters in the Bible who encountered God and were never the same. One of the greatest transformations was in the life of Saul. On the road to persecuting the Christians in Damascus, Saul (who eventually became the apostle Paul) encountered God. The experience left him temporarily blind and dependent on those he was going to persecute. He went on to become the most prominent apostle in taking the message of the Gospel to the world. He wrote a major part of the New Testament. After his encounter with God, Paul speaks about growth in Colossians 2:19. He writes,

> *"[Hold fast to the head,] from whom the whole body, supported and held together by its ligaments and sinews, grows as God causes it to grow."*

This passage shows us a key truth about growth: that it is up to God, not us, to make things grow. Let me give you an example.

I have a friend who decided that she was going to grow green beans. So, she pulled out the only gardening book that she owned and read all about the different types of green beans and what kind of environment helps them to grow. Then, she bought the beans themselves and read the planting instructions carefully. She tilled the soil, planted the beans, and even mulched all around them to keep out the weeds. If it didn't rain for a few days, she would pull out the hose and water the beans. She did all she could to help the beans grow. But at the end of the day, she was not capable of causing the beans to grow. She would sit by her window at night, looking out at the garden and wish with all of her might that she could make her beans grow—but she couldn't do it. She could plant and water them, but only God could make them grow.

This same principle applies to our lives.

There is no magic pill for Christian growth; there is no program that creates growth. As wonderful as any new spiritual habit, study, sermon series, teacher, or book can be, none of these things are what grows us. They are doing nothing more than planting or watering a seed—the growing itself comes from God (1 Corinthians 3:6)! Many Christians are mystified about how to grow. Into our confusion, God simply says,

"Abide in me. Grow in me. Those who live in me will grow and apart from me there is no growth."

Questions:

1. Do you think growing will require big changes in your life?

2. How might those changes affect the way you live?

3. Why is growth so important?

4. What sort of watering or tilling might you do that will result in growth?

5. What discipline might serve to plant you so that God might bring growth to your life?

Day 2 – Healthy Growth
Read: John 15:1-6

When my son was three years old, he came to me with a concern. He wanted to be bigger. He said to me, "Daddy, I want to grow, but I can't." He strained and stretched and looked at himself. "See, Daddy, I can't grow." He was very disappointed to learn that we can't make ourselves grow.

I told him, "God makes us grow." I went on to explain, "We need to focus on being healthy: eating healthy food, sleeping when Mommy and Daddy say so, and playing a lot." He believed me, but I could tell that he wasn't satisfied. He wanted to know three easy steps to grow three inches or, even better, find the right person who could make him grow overnight. We know human growth does not happen that way. There are things that we can do to impair growth, and there are moments in our lives when growth happens easily, but human growth is something that we can only influence; it is beyond our total control. These same principles apply to our spiritual growth.

On the other hand, there is much that will stunt growth. If we don't water plants, trim them, or control the weeds, the plants may not grow to full size and produce a fullness of fruit. In fact, they may actually die for lack of water, or be choked out by weeds. In our personal lives, neglecting to read God's Word, to fellowship with his people, and to pray will prevent us from growing. God's way of "trimming" us is to allow adversity to come into our lives. If we turn away from Him during those times or strike back in an unhealthy way, we will fail to grow and may still have to learn the lesson at another time and through other circumstances.

Nevertheless, a life without growth is not life. If you are not growing in your spiritual life you are wilting. There is no standing still, no flat ground. It is either up or down toward reaching spiritual maturity. In the same way, growth is essential to your personal well-being, growth is an essential characteristic of a healthy church. While the church cannot manufacture growth, the spiritual growth of people will naturally result in the growth of the church. Many of the churches in the U.S. and around the world are failing to grow. So, how can we see growth?

The key to growth is trusting continually in the work of Jesus in our daily lives. If you doubt that He is and that He cares about your life, you will either give up or try to succeed on your own strength. It is common to think that all you have to do is keep all the rules, but God wants you to yield yourself up and live each day in a relationship with Him, leaning on His love and grace. This means that you do not take offense when others disappoint you, that you allow room for others to make mistakes, and that you show kindness even to those who are undeserving. Turn all these things over to Christ. In prayer, give them to Him and let Him deal with the offender. As you do these things, you will find that they become easier each day. Soon you will find the spirit of anger leaving you, that gentleness and self-control are new characteristics others will see in your life.

Questions:

1. What are the obstacles to growth that you see in your life? How could they be removed?

2. What will happen if you try to keep the rules without the power of Jesus?

3. What are three offenses against you that you need to forgive?

4. In what way is your incarceration adversity that God is using to help you grow?

5. Discuss this with your mentor.

Day 3 – Maturity
Read: John 1:40-42

Little children are known for their fascination with superheroes. They will often try to dress like them, talk like them and will sometimes even try to imitate their superpowers. But no matter how hard they try, deep down, they know they will never be able to morph into those they admire. I think as adults we sometimes take the same view of many of the men and women of the Bible. We look up to them and want to imitate their actions, but we struggle to truly believe that we will ever be able to follow Christ to the degree that they did. But here is the beautiful thing: God works in our lives in the same way that God worked in theirs so many years ago. We really aren't that different! In the same way that God was constantly growing them, God is constantly growing us. In order to better understand this truth, let's take a closer look at God's constant hand in the growth process of one of Christ's disciples. A look at Peter's life reveals a great deal about Christian growth. Peter's life illustrates that all of us need to grow and that God will use us even as we are growing. Second, it reveals that growth is a lengthy process. Peter was always growing—he was a work in progress. Even after he began to lead the early church, he was still growing. God and other church leaders confronted and instructed him so that he would continue to grow in maturity. Like all Christians, Peter's growth began when he heard and accepted the call to follow Christ. Those first weeks and months must have been exciting beyond imagination. His brother Andrew introduced him to Jesus (John 1:42). In short order, he witnessed his first miracle after a night of unsuccessful fishing (Luke 5:4–8). He committed to following Christ and witnessed the healing of his mother-in-law (Matthew 4:18–20; Mark 1:29–31). It would be hard to overestimate the amount of growing Peter did. He left his job and home to find out more about Jesus.

Peter seems to have taken giant steps in growth during Jesus' early ministry. Certainly, he joins the disciples in their foolishness on many occasions, but he also sets himself apart through his singular faith. With James and John, he is invited into Jesus' inner circle to witness the resurrection of a little girl (Mark 5:37–42). When the disciples encounter Jesus walking on water, Peter asks to join Christ and gets out of the boat. Now, to be sure, after only a few steps across the water, he loses faith and begins to sink, but we would be mistaken not to notice that Peter is the only one who steps out. Christ identifies his doubt, but it is doubt mixed with faith (Matthew 14:22–31).

Peter also grows in boldness in his relationship with Christ through Christ's teaching. When he hears a parable that he does not understand, he is courageous and speaks up and asks what it means (Matthew 15:15). At a peak of understanding and leadership, Peter proclaims, "You are the Messiah, the Son of the living God." Christ (which means Messiah or anointed one) responds that he is blessed (Matthew 16:16).

From this point in the story, it would be easy to imagine that Peter had made it. The mistaken conclusion is that Peter had grown into the perfect follower of Christ. Peter was far from being perfect. As Christ's ministry turns toward the sacrifice on the cross, Peter is less and less ready to follow and repeatedly finds himself in conflict with Christ's mission. Not long after Peter proclaims that Jesus is the Christ, Peter rebukes Jesus and tries to prevent Him from suffering on the cross, and Jesus responds by calling him Satan (Matthew 16:21–23).

When Jesus miraculously transfigures and shows Peter, James, and John a glimpse of his heavenly nature, Peter makes a fool of himself (Matthew 17:1–6). At the final Passover with Jesus, he makes grand claims of loyalty that he cannot back up (Matthew 26:33). In the garden, he sleeps when Jesus asks him to stay awake and pray (Matthew 26:37–41). Most dramatically, as Jesus is on trial for his life, Peter stands outside and denies ever having known him (Matthew 26:69–70). How could one so close to Jesus fall so far? How could he have so much faith in Jesus' power but none in Jesus' purpose? Peter goes to the empty tomb and meets the risen Lord (John 20). However, he still returns to fishing, unsure of what to do (John 21:3). Jesus confronts Peter and calls him back to Christ's service (John 21:15–19). Even after Jesus ascends to heaven, Peter grows in his faith little by little. Peter preaches boldly in Jerusalem and leads the church well. Nonetheless, he resists God's intention to include the Gentiles in salvation. Paul has to confront him because Peter stops eating with non-Jews. From the beginning of Peter's faith journey to the end, he is growing in his walk.

Christian maturity is not a destination at which one arrives. It is a direction in which one moves. The story of Peter's growth in faithfulness and his tragic failures, even when one would think he would know better, is no different than the story of our lives today. We can relate to a man like Peter. Like him, we are constantly growing. May we continue following Christ on this growth path until that day in eternity when we will be completely mature.

Questions:

1. Which part of Peter's growth is most inspiring to you?

2. Which story of Peter's human foolishness is most similar to something that has happened to you?

3. How does this study of Peter's failures encourage you in your walk with God?

Day 4 – Worship
Read: Romans 12:1-2

The church sign said, "Worship Service at 11:00." For many people, "worship" means this: you put on special clothes, set aside your daily "To Do" list, leave home at 10:45, and drive to the church building. You find a parking spot and then a place to sit in the worship area. After some songs, a sermon, and, of course, an offering, you file out to your car and head home. Worship is over. Back to the real world. Right? Not according to the Scriptures. For those walking with Jesus, worship is the real world, and it encompasses our entire lives. It's more than something we do for an hour or so one day of the week. God has created us to worship in everything we say and do. Maybe you've heard the saying, "Your life is God's gift to you. What you do with it is your gift back to God." That pretty well describes whole-life worship: the gift of your life, laid out and lived out before God.

This concept of whole-life worship is described in Romans 12. For eleven chapters Paul has pointed to the incredible goodness and grace of God—creating us, sending Jesus to rescue us, forgiving us, giving us new life and eternal hope. Then, as if drawing a line under all this, he sums up the only sensible response from us in the reading for today. He urges us to offer our bodies as living sacrifices, holy and pleasing to God. This is our true worship.

The image of sacrifices being offered in worship was familiar to the Jewish believers. They were accustomed to sacrificing animals on the altar before God. But now Paul says that God isn't interested in the sacrifice of animals. What He really wants, what is truly pleasing and holy before Him, is YOU. Our best and most spiritual act of worship is not mere religious ritual in a sacred worship space but rather the offering of our very selves back to God in everyday life. It's as if we climb willingly onto the altar, look up, and say to God, "Here I am. I belong to you. I offer my entire life for your purposes," a living sacrifice. The problem with living sacrifices is they have a tendency to keep crawling off the altar!

It's a lot less demanding if we can compartmentalize our relationship with God and keep it pinned down to a few hours here or there. It's rather easy to donate our time on Sunday morning for church worship. Don't misunderstand. Our corporate worship times are extremely important to God. It is a collective time to bring gifts to God, give Him our thanks and praise, to confess and repent. When we come together for worship, it's about Him, not about you or me. It is like a bridal shower where everyone blesses the guest of honor with thoughtful gifts.

But, worshipping God involves more than a Sunday worship service. Whole life worship brings us into God's presence so that God is part of our lives every day, all the time. So,

"Whatever you do, whether in word or deed, do it all in the name of the Lord Jesus, giving thanks to God the Father through Him."

Worship is also attributing worth to God. It is honoring Him in the way we live. It is thanking Him for his daily provision, giving of our money in support of His Kingdom, and praising Him for who He is and for what He has done. No part of our daily living should fail to honor Him. When we crawl out of bed each morning, the first thing we must do is crawl right onto the altar of self-sacrifice. He has given you life for another day. Offer it back to Him as a gift that will please Him. That's what whole-life worship is about.

Questions:

1. When you hear the word worship, what activities usually come to your mind first?

2. How can you begin to think of all kinds of daily activities as ways to worship?

3. What is the greatest obstacle in your life to whole-life worship?

Day 5 – Devotions
Read: II Timothy 3:16

Joe didn't bother to look at a map before he jumped in the car. He printed out Map-Quest directions, grabbed his keys, and flew out the door. His driving went fine until he realized he had somehow left behind the second page of his directions. His one sheet of navigation instructions had steered him into a maze of one-way streets and left him there in the dark of night. Now he was downtown, turned around, and downright lost. Why hadn't he invested in that GPS?! Why didn't he keep a map in the glove compartment?! And why couldn't he bring himself to call and ask his wife for help?! We can all identify with Joe. Everyone gets lost now and then. And God knows that we can easily lose our way in life, too. Knowing where we are and where to go next isn't always easy.

Fortunately, God always points the way forward in our walk with Jesus. God provides directions. The writer of Psalm 119:105 rejoices,

"Your word is a lamp to my feet and a light for my path."

God gives us special high-beam headlights of truth to guide us through life: the light of Scripture. This great book called the Bible is a beautiful gift. It tells the story of God's care for all people through time. Its pages are filled with ordinary human beings, and yet it is breathed into life by God. Show me a Christian who is growing, and I'll show you a Christian who is taking in the Scriptures. Apart from these words of life, we remain stuck. Ignorance of the Scriptures is ignorance of Christ. To walk with Jesus, we need at least a basic understanding of Scripture. Studying the Bible more deeply allows us to become disciples who are healthy and mature.

Unfortunately, many find the Bible daunting or murky. Maybe a modern translation like the NLT will help. Also, a commitment to dig in will yield life-changing rewards where you will find that Scripture is anything but dull. It is through the pages of Scripture that we hear the voice of God. Instead of wondering what God thinks of me, I hear God say,

"I love you so much I sent my son to save you." (John 3:16)

When I doubt there is any purpose for my life, God says, "I know the plans I have for you" (Jeremiah 29:11). Ask God to plant in your heart a desire to study the Bible. Ask God to make it real and understandable so He can light the way forward for you. Here are some helpful guides as you dig into God's Word.

Make a plan and do it. There is no substitute for having a pattern of behavior and sticking to it.

Study alone and study with others. Christians need time alone with God's Word. Private reading, however, bears its greatest fruit when coupled with group study. In this group context you are protected from the error of misunderstanding and are able to share the fruit of private study.

Be honest. Do not search the Scriptures to support your belief, but look for the whole truth on a subject whether you agree with it or not.

Do not pick and choose. This means that we cannot pull one verse (or even one book) out of the Bible and expect to be able to read it accurately or faithfully. Take the whole Bible in context.

Consider: Who wrote it, to whom was it written, and what were the circumstances? A commentary can be very helpful.

Where the Bible speaks, we speak. Where the Bible is silent, we are silent. There are things that the Bible does not tell us. I cannot let myself say more than the Bible does. This is a hard rule to follow, but it is an important one. A person growing as a disciple must submit to Scripture, both to what it says and to what it does not say.

Questions and activities:

1. Being serious about Scripture leads to spiritual strength, and not being serious about it leads to spiritual weakness. What situations in your own life reflect these statements?

2. What are ways that studying as part of a group helps our understanding of Scripture?

3. What are some resources you could use to find out more about the background of the Scriptures?

4. Pray that God will help you understand what you read and give you a hunger for His Word.

5. If you are struggling with understanding the translation you are using, try finding a modern translation. Talk to your mentor about this.

Day 6 - Prayer
Read: Matthew 6:9–13

Prayer is a very broad topic, and many books have been written on the subject. We can only briefly cover it in this devotional. Simply stated, prayer is communication with God. It should be as natural as a conversation with a friend. It doesn't have to be a great-sounding oratory. Many Christians are intimidated by prayer because they fear they do not have the right words. Prayer has been fittingly described as the breath of the Christian life. Just as physical life is dependent on breathing air, spiritual life is dependent on the breath of prayer.

We were designed for communication with God, and therefore, we were designed for prayer. God longs to be close to us so that we might be transformed and re-created. All of this happens in prayer. Nevertheless, struggling with prayer is the norm for most Christians. Many people do not pray at all or very little. Some Christians only pray during times of need. Then, after the present distress is over, they are again silent. Others are inclined to pray only when things are going well. In order to have a real relationship with God we must be faithful to pray at all times and in all places.

Jesus knew how important prayer was, and consequently, He spent a great deal of His ministry praying and teaching about prayer. To become people of prayer, we should study His example, His teaching, and the model for prayer that He has given, as you saw in the reading for this devotion. Jesus prayed alone and in public (Luke 5:16; Matthew 6:9). He prayed in thanksgiving and in pain (Matthew 14:19; Luke 22:44). He prayed in the face of temptation and in the comfort of friends (Matthew 26:36-39; Luke 11:1). He prayed as the day began and as the day ended (Mark 1:35; Matthew 4:23). He prayed for children and for His enemies (Matthew 19:13; Luke 23:34). He prayed for Himself, He prayed for God's will, and in John 17, He prayed for us. He was thinking about you in that prayer.

We must realize that in every moment prayer is fitting. Fear, crisis, and uncertainty should lead us to pray. James reminds us, "Is anyone among you in trouble, they should pray" (James 5:13). But Jesus' example indicates that waking up in the morning is reason enough to pray (Mark 6:46). Facing the day, the crowds, family, and friends; whatever the day required was a reason to pray. Eating a meal, especially one shared with others, is a reason to pray (Luke 24:30). Trust that God will cause growth to happen in you, and you will grow in prayer. Perhaps you wonder why we need to go to God in prayer since God already knows everything, including our needs. Prayer is more important for us than for God. It is a demonstration of our faith that we actually expect God to act on our requests. Prayer empowers and appropriates God's participation in the natural order. God doesn't force Himself on us, but prayer is our invitation to Him, especially on behalf of other's needs. Prayer demonstrates our dependence on Him to meet our needs and carry our burdens. Prayer should be considered an awesome opportunity to move the hands of the greatest power in the universe.

Questions:

1. What holds you back from praying more?

2. Do you pray in times of trouble or when all is well?

3. What is your favorite setting for prayer?

4. How can you arrange your schedule with that setting in mind?

Additional reading: *This Present Darkness* by Frank Peretti

Day 7 - Attitude of Gratitude
Read: Philippians 4:10-14

"I complained about having no shoes until I met a man who had no feet." This short phrase expresses the core of a grateful heart. I was curious as to where it came from, so I searched the internet. I discovered that it originated with Sheikh Muslih-uddin Sa'di Shirazi, as recorded in The <u>Gulistan of Sa'di,</u> composed in the year 1258. (Now try to remember that!) The opposite of this premise is seeing the abundance of others and feeling we are somehow entitled to the same benefits for ourselves. This latter error is the root of ingratitude that so dramatically affects society of this century. I hear it every day in media advertising that goes like this, "You deserve a break today." Such self-serving thinking results in jealousy and anger. It leads to theft, hatred, and violence. In many respects, it plays a part in the depression that captivates so many people. How can the advertising people know who deserves a break, anyway?

Ingratitude starts with independence from God. Romans 1:21 says,

"Although they knew God, they did not glorify Him as God, nor were thankful, but became futile in their thoughts..."

The next step is to reject the authority of the family and seek independence. We put our confidence in our own resources. When we depend entirely on ourselves, then we have no need to be thankful to others. The third step takes place when we look at what others have and believe that we are entitled to have the same things. This is often the message of our culture, but it stands in total opposition to what the Bible teaches.

Part of growing in Christ is an appreciation for what we have. We are to recognize Him as the giver of all things, the source of our real needs. We are not supposed to compare ourselves with others and the things they have. Two of the Ten Commandments deal with this subject; "You shall not covet" and "You shall not steal." Both of these sins come from the desire to have what belongs to others. People whose lives are spared during great tragedies realize that things are expendable, but life is precious beyond comparison.

Ungrateful people grumble and constantly complain about their own wants and needs. They are never satisfied with what they have. They continually desire to have more possessions. There is never enough to satisfy the desires of the flesh. These are unhappy people out to serve themselves and have no compassion for the wants and needs of others. They fail to see the meaning of life. Such people are unattractive and often find themselves without friends.

God has not called us to live this way. He came that we might have life and have it more abundantly. He warns us not to be controlled by materialism and the desires of the flesh. We are to be detached from the nonessentials of this life and to focus instead on spiritual qualities. We are to look at life from God's point of view. Live in contentment, get priorities straight, and live in accordance with God's purpose for life.

Questions:

1. What do you believe is God's purpose for your life?

2. Discuss your purpose with your mentor.

3. In what ways are you ungrateful?

4. How would you describe the abundant life?

5. What can you do to develop a grateful heart?

STUDY 6 – REACH

Day 1 – God Reaches Out to Us

"Then the man and his wife heard the sound of the LORD God as he was walking in the garden in the cool of the day, and they hid from the LORD God among the trees of the garden. But the LORD God called to the man, 'Where are you?'" Genesis 3:8,9

God created man for fellowship with Him. From the very beginning of creation, before the fall, God fellowshipped with Adam and Eve face to face. After Adam and Eve ate from the forbidden tree, they knew they had sinned, so they hid themselves in the garden. They realized that fellowship had been broken by their own disobedience. We can see the same response in our pets when they understand they have been disobedient. Our dog will hide from us and be afraid to approach us when he has done something wrong. Just like God, when He didn't see Adam and Eve waiting for Him, we called out to the dog, "Where are you?" We know immediately that he has been disobedient.

Because mankind became sinful, our Holy God could no longer have that face-to-face intimacy with them. He cast them out of the garden that He had prepared for them, but He never stopped loving them. He reached out to them and continues reaching out to us. This is clearly demonstrated in the stage play "*In the Beginning*," presented at the Sight and Sound Auditorium located in Lancaster, PA. God provides for their needs and blesses them in many ways. They spoke to their children often about the wonders of God and the garden where they once lived.

Christ's coming is the ultimate expression of His reaching out to us. God came in human form to restore the fellowship that we had broken. God sent Jesus to be the second Adam. The first Adam was disobedient but Christ was obedient even unto death. Satan set out to destroy God's creation, and he thought that by destroying Jesus on the cross, he could prevent Jesus from reaching out to all mankind. As C.S. Lewis so aptly states in "*The Lion, the Witch, and the Wardrobe,*" the Witch (Satan) didn't know about the deeper secrets of the universe, "When a willing victim who had committed no treachery was killed in a traitor's stead, the Table would crack and Death itself would start working backward." Jesus' sacrifice redeemed us from the curse of the law!

Having been reached by God and inspired by Christ's example, we reach out to others. To develop this habit, we cultivate three skills: inviting, welcoming, and living. The practice of inviting is the consistent offer of inclusion to those around us. On Christ's behalf, we extend the offer to be included in the work that God is doing and to be redeemed and formed into a community. Welcoming is the practice of including those who have accepted our invitation. As others are willing, we integrate them into our lives, we accommodate their needs, and we care for their weaknesses. We demonstrate our willingness to let "*my*" church and "*my*" small group and "*my*" home become truly "*our*" church and "*our*" group and "*our*" home. Living a life that is attractive is the habit of living in the world in such a way that God is glorified and the world is mystified. When we follow Christ and live our lives for others, the world will wonder. The ones we seek will come to us, longing to be included and welcomed into the kingdom.

Questions:

1. Why is it easier to invite someone to a baseball game or a concert than to church?

2. Why is Christian evangelism so detested by our culture?

3. What could you do to create in your life a heart that is seeking and loving other people?

4. How can you develop the three practices of reaching (inviting, welcoming, and living) in your life?

5. What would it look like for you to follow Christ in these reaching practices? Try to be specific.

Day 2 – God Reaches Out to Others
Read: Colossians 1:13-14

Several years ago, Ray Charles popularized a song entitled *"Georgia on My Mind."* I'm not sure if that was just a catchy phrase or if Georgia really did fill his thoughts. Have you ever considered what is on God's mind? You are. I am. God's mind is on people. God's heart is concerned with people. The religious leaders of Jesus' day criticized Him for His habit of socializing with sinners. He responded by telling parables. The following teaching stories are very revealing about the heart and mind of God.

Read Luke 15:4–10.

God's heart is especially focused on the lost. Jesus makes it clear that it is not an accident that He socializes with sinners. He has come to do the will of the Father. He has specifically chosen to give His attention to those farthest from God. Beneath the simplicity of these parables lie a variety of powerful truths. First, we must notice that from the perspective of God, all people were once His. The shepherd is not hunting for just any sheep or hoping to find some sheep. It is the shepherd's own sheep that has been lost. Likewise, the woman is not a treasure hunter. She is not scouring the beach with a metal detector. She is looking for what was once her possession. God thinks of us with this same perspective. Christ is urgently seeking to save the lost. Even when we do not acknowledge it, the Father acknowledges that we are His children and longs to restore us to His family.

The second great truth of these parables is that God and Christ have made a choice to focus on the lost. God's mission is to reach those still outside of the kingdom to draw them into meaningful relationships with Him.

The third great truth is found in the nature of the hunt. In both cases, it is a hunt "until he/she finds it." God's pursuit is not shallow or halfhearted. It is a whole-hearted search with immense passion. When the search is successful, the celebration begins. Again, we must not miss the detail that this is no mild celebration; it is a great party, an angelic celebration. Jesus completes our understanding of God's heart with another parable.

Read Luke 15:11–32

In this parable, Jesus gives a gripping image of God's outreaching love. The errant son thought that his father's wealth was the most valuable thing he had. He takes the money and breaks the relationship. When he runs out of stuff, he goes back, not seeking a relationship but seeking employment. The father cares only about the relationship. He is not concerned about financial or material equity; he is concerned about a restored relationship. In the same way, God reaches out to us, the lost children, not to settle a score or secure a debt but to restore a relationship. There is a third character in the parable of the forgiving father. The elder brother does not share his father's values. He values fairness and equity. This character is a warning to those who are a part of God's family. Each of us is called to share the Father's passion to seek those far from Him and celebrate when they are found.

Questions:

1. One of the truths from the parables is that God's pursuit is wholehearted and unending. What evidence do you have from your own life that God doesn't give up?

2. To whom are you reaching out with the kind of wholeheartedness God has? If you can't think of anyone, what do you need to change in your schedule or priorities?

3. To what degree does your church share God's passion to reach the gospel? What indicators of this do you see?

Day 3 – The Organized Church, God's Tool for Reaching Out
Read: Acts 13:1–3

A large, thriving church located in the region's capital was known for its excellent leadership. They were racially diverse, multi-talented, and highly trained. Its two most notable leaders were a renowned biblical scholar and a leader known for his generosity and encouragement. The church was in the midst of an ongoing fast and prayer meeting. No one knows why. Maybe it was just their regular practice. In the midst of this, God put it on the heart of the community to send out their two best leaders so that these two might go and share the Gospel with the rest of the nation. The whole congregation gathered together and fasted and prayed and gave these men and their companions the necessary resources to leave and go tell others about what Jesus had done. Years would pass before these men would return to the brave and bold visionaries they left behind in Antioch. This is the story told in today's reading.

This is exactly the way Jesus intended for the church to act. In every case, the values and character of God should be present in the character of the church. God is always seeking those far away. God wants the church to be seeking in the same way. To do this, the church must turn its gaze beyond itself just like the church did in Antioch. Each Christian and each local congregation must choose to think less about its own needs and more about the needs of those who have not yet heard and believed the news of Christ. The first actions of Christ's ministry were to invite people to walk with Him. His community of followers just seemed to grow: 12, then 20, then 70, then 120. Five hundred were following close enough that they saw Christ after the resurrection (1 Corinthians 15:6). As the community of Christ's followers moved in the world, it drew more people like a snowball rolling downhill. Even after Jesus is gone, this pattern continues. The church is continually opening itself to receive those streaming into the kingdom and reaching out to those far away.

Christ expected that the church would be a place of refuge for all people. Jesus always envisioned that many people from all backgrounds would be reached by the church and find a home. Then, having found a home, they would, in turn, begin reaching out to others. The real outreach to the world can only be accomplished through organization. But the church's ability to reach out as God calls will be determined by its ability to develop one crucial practice. Christians must develop friendships and live in a community with those who are not Christians. If the church creates for itself an enclosed circle of relationships, then Christians will never even meet the very people Christ came to save.

Read Luke 5:27–32

This was certainly the wrong sort of party for a new rabbi to attend. Yet this is exactly where Jesus shows up. The church today must find itself in the same situation. It is for the "wrong sort" of people that the church exists. Just as a hospital exists for the sick, the church exists for the broken and lost. If you are a part of the kingdom but not associating with those far from the kingdom, you are not yet reaching. The church that has closed itself off from the community and the people around it is not the church Jesus wanted to create. Jesus came to create a church that is salt and light to the world (Matthew 5:13–16). You are called to be that church.

Questions:

1. How does this change your idea about the church?

2. How can you begin reaching out to others?

3. What might be holding you back from outreach?

4. Make plans with your mentor about what church you will attend.

5. Discuss with your mentor some ways in which you can participate in a ministry of reaching others.

Day 4 – Start Where You Are
Read: Acts 6:1–6; 8:26-40

He is not the star of any book of the Bible. He was not one of the special twelve disciples or a general or king or prophet. His first job was an unpopular administrative job. He received the job because the disciples were too busy. He was not a trained preacher or evangelist. He had not gone to Bible college. Despite all this, he is known today under the name Philip the Evangelist, and his ministry was a dynamic catalyst for the growth of the church. During the growth of the church in Acts, trouble was brewing because the needs of the widows and poor were growing faster than the church's benevolence ministry could keep up. Also, the church is becoming culturally more diverse. The leadership is largely native to Jerusalem, and many new Christian converts are from the wider Roman world. Consequently, these new Christians felt slighted in the daily distribution of provisions.

The church chose seven capable men to oversee this growing controversy. They took on a difficult task, facing what could have become the first church split. Philip was one of these new deacons but lost his new job soon after he accepted it. After Stephen was martyred, a great persecution arose in Jerusalem, targeting these foreign-born Christians. Philip and many others were driven from the city. This persecution is recorded in the eighth chapter of Acts. Even as they fled persecution for their faith, they continued to proclaim the good news. I suppose, had they consulted me, I might have advised them to lay low for a while.

On the contrary, Luke (the author of Acts) wants us to recognize that this persecution was an opportunity for the church and not an obstacle. As the verse continues, Luke relates a general truth that those scattered by the persecution shared the Good News of Jesus wherever they went (Acts 8:4). In the remainder of the chapter, we see how this truth was embodied in the life of Philip.

Philip flees to Samaria. For someone who wanted to hide, it was a safe place. The Samaritans had little respect for the Jewish religious establishment, and the Roman government's presence was strong, which would protect him from religious violence. Philip was not someone who wanted to hide. He received no special call to evangelism. He was the same person he had been when he was selected as a gifted administrator, but Philip was a man who did what needed doing. In Jerusalem, the church needed Greek-speaking, administratively gifted food distributors, so he took on that challenge. In Samaria, they had not heard the Good News of Christ, so naturally it spills out in his everyday interactions with other people.

Finally, in Acts 8:26, Philip receives direction from the Holy Spirit to go down the road from Jerusalem to Gaza. As he went, he met an Ethiopian eunuch, an influential officer of the queen of Ethiopia. Philip was able to explain the ancient text that predicts Jesus' sacrificial death. Upon hearing this good news, the Ethiopian is baptized. The Spirit miraculously snatches away Philip. He appears at Azotus and then travels, eventually arriving in Caesarea, and he continues to share as he goes. In Matthew 28:18-20 Christ gave His last instructions to His disciples, saying,

"All authority in heaven and on earth has been given to me.
Therefore [as you are going] make disciples of all nations,
baptizing them in the name of the Father and of the Son and of
the Holy Spirit, and teaching them to obey everything I have
commanded you. And surely, I am with you always, to the very
end of the age."

We sometimes interpret this as two commands: the command to "go" and the command to "make disciples." In fact, it is a singular command to make disciples "as you are going." Philip is a perfect example of this teaching. He never set out on a missionary journey. He was never commissioned as an evangelist. Rather, he found that as he was fleeing or traveling, or going wherever God sent him, he had opportunities to share what he had and make disciples, baptizing and teaching. Just like Phillip, you are going places, and in all of those places are people God longs to reach. You are God's reaching arms.

Questions:

1. How does knowing Philip's background in a "non-missionary" role (food distributor) broaden our perspective on what kind of people the Spirit uses to make more disciples?

2. Do you "naturally" tell people you know the good news about your family, your hobbies, and other parts of life?

3. Do you "naturally" tell people you know about Jesus?

4. Why is it harder to talk to others about Jesus?

Day 5 – Invitation
Read: John 4:1-24

I met him in my first week of college. We had two classes together and had similar academic interests. Over the next four years, we had at least two classes together every semester except one. We co-founded a singing group; we shared the same campus job. He and I studied together two nights a week. We talked about our families and our childhood. He asked me about my faith, and I answered when he asked.

He and I built a friendship. In four years, I never invited him to a single Christian event. I didn't invite him to church with me, or to my small group, or the campus worship service, or to our beach trip; nothing!

Ten years have passed since college. He and I have exchanged three e-mails in those ten years. Each one was a commonly distributed birth announcement. For four years I was waiting for the right opportunity. I imagined that I was building my friendship capital so when I did decide to invite him, he would be ready to accept. That isn't a bad theory, but I realize now that my real problem was selfishness. I was more concerned with maintaining the fun of our friendship than telling my friend about Christ.

Christians who are committed to Christ and His teaching will be reaching out. They will invite others along with them on the journey. To invite someone to share in a Christian community is not being pushy; it is being kind. Giving someone a chance to grow in their relationship with Christ is the supreme act of friendship. The central questions are: have you found something worth sharing, and are you willing to share it?

In the fourth chapter of John, we read about a most wonderful encounter. Jesus meets a woman at a well. He engages her in conversation and reveals Himself to her as the Messiah. She is tough. The woman at the well challenges His ideas and questions His motives. She is well-educated and not easily convinced. But she knows that she has discovered something. She knows that this man, who can reveal things about her past and claims to be the Messiah, is something special. Even the rudeness of Jesus' disciples cannot deter her interest. John records,

"Then, leaving her water jar, the woman went back to the town and said to the people, 'Come, see a man who told me everything I ever did. Could this be the Messiah?' They came out of the town and made their way toward him."

A few verses later, John summarizes the consequence of this encounter.

"Many of the Samaritans from that town believed in him because of the woman's testimony, 'He told me everything I ever did.' So, when the Samaritans came to him, they urged him to stay with them, and he stayed for two days. And because of his words, many more became believers. They said to the woman, 'We no longer believe just because of what you said; now we have heard for ourselves, and we know that this man really is the Savior of the world.'"

This is the power of an invitation. The invitation does not need to be perfect and the inviter does not need to be sure of all things. She understood that she did not need to convince them about who Jesus was; she needed only to invite them. Her testimony was sufficient for them to accept the invitation, but their full faith came from their own meeting with Christ. Once again, when she invited the whole town to come meet Jesus, she was not yet convinced that Jesus was the long-awaited Christ. She was sure that she had met someone amazing, and she wanted others to meet him. Similarly, our ability to invite is not limited by what we don't know. We can always invite you to what we know.

I have met many people who feel that their ignorance is an obstacle to inviting others. Christians wonder how they can invite a friend to join them when they don't have all the answers. Christians wonder if it is appropriate to invite others when they themselves are still searching or doubtful. To all of these, I would recommend the story of the man born blind. I have many times used a variation on his words, "Whether this particular opinion or fact is true or not I don't know. But this one thing I know…"

God has placed people in your life that need to be invited. They do not need an argument; they need an invitation. I pray that you will not miss any opportunity to say, "Come and see what I have seen."

Questions:

1. Is there someone you wish you had invited to come and hear the Word of Jesus? What held you back from inviting them?

2. How might you reconnect with that person?

3. What aspect of the story of the woman at the well is most helpful to you in overcoming your hesitancy to inviting them?

Day 6 – Welcome
Read: 1 Corinthians 9:22-27

I entered the bicycle shop with great anticipation. I was finally ready to buy a good bike. I was in my late twenties, still riding the bike I got at 14. I had heard that over the years, bikes had gotten lighter, faster, and in every way better. I had saved enough money, or so I thought, to finally buy myself a good bike from a real bike shop. The shopkeeper asked, "Can I help you?"

"Yes, I would like to buy a bike."

"Wonderful, what kind of bike do you need."

"I don't know, exactly." His eyes sunk, but I continued, "I want something mainly just to tool around on the roads, but I like to ride trails some, too." He started to move back to whatever he had been doing. "So, you're not a cyclist?"

I wasn't sure what to say, so I said, "Uh, I used to ride a lot as a kid." His back was completely turned now, "We really cater more to serious cyclists, but you're welcome to look around."

I left.

I call that attitude the "ski shop mentality," although clearly, it is prevalent at many specialty shops. I often get it at plumbing supply stores when I tell them that I need three more "thingys" just like the one I have. I often wish they would just have a sign on the door: "If you intend to shop here, you had better know what you are doing. We don't have time for novices." Such a sign would save me a great deal of embarrassment.

I eventually found a better bike shop. The sixteen-year-old behind the counter was thrilled that I was buying my first real bike. He asked me what I was riding now, and when I told him, he exclaimed, "Oh, you are going to love this." I told him my budget, and in a flash, he tracked down 6 bikes of varying styles and sizes and hauled them outside. He said, "Here, go ride for a while. Feel free to ride down the street a mile or two so you can get a feel for the gears and derailleur. Some of these new designs don't work for everybody. I'll be inside."

I rode around for a while. He was right; it was wonderful! I had entered a new world. I felt like a cyclist. When I got back to the store, needless to say, I bought the bike. Such is the power of welcoming. As followers of Christ, we are called to be welcoming, and not just to those who are already on the way. I know why that first shop owner didn't want to deal with me. He couldn't sell a bike to me the way he would to a cyclist. I didn't know what any of the fancy words meant. I wouldn't provide lots of repeat business for gadgets like a cyclist would. In contrast, at the second shop I was included. The young salesman was not just willing but actually thrilled to help me ride my first good bike.

The church must always guard against being a specialty shop. We can so quickly develop our own language. We can so quickly forget how foreign and intimidating it was to first walk into a church building. Some of us grew up in the church and never walked in for the first time. We may think that we are welcoming, but really, we are only welcoming to other Christians. We may think that we are reaching out, but really, we are only reaching out to those like us.

Read: 1 Corinthians 6:9–11

What a powerful text. It starts out a little harsh, doesn't it.? It sounds like Paul is saying that all these people are unwelcome in the church, but then he surprises us. He reminds them that this is what they once were. He is precisely telling them that the church if it is reaching out the way Jesus did, welcomes those who don't seem to belong yet. In fact, the more someone seems not to belong, the more the church must intentionally welcome. You are called to the practice of welcoming. You could become a specialty shop. You could greet only those you already know. You could talk to only those who are like you racially and economically. You could associate only with those who have "cleaned up" their lives on the outside. You could tell all those who come looking for Jesus, "We're really a church for

Christians." Or you could practice the art of welcoming. You could recognize that the church exists for those not yet a part of it. You could recognize that however far from God a person is, so once were you. You could say to them, "I am so glad you are here. You will not believe what I get to share with you. You are going to love this place."

Questions:

1. When have you felt the most welcome as a visitor at a church?

2. What did they do to make you feel welcome?

3. What type of people does your surrounding community consider

4. "Outcast?"

5. What could a church do to make them feel welcome?

Day 7 – It's More Than Words
Read: 1 Peter 2:11–17

For five months they had shared Saturday breakfasts at Denny's. Neither could remember who invited whom the first time, but it quickly became their tradition. Phil had been praying for a way to reach out to Brett, his next-door neighbor. Some driveway conversations led to a friendship and a discovery that they shared a common interest in Harleys. Without Phil having to plan it, they were eating together every week. Long after the grits and gravy were gone, the coffee and conversation flowed. They talked about kids, careers, motorcycles, and vacations. Over time Brett opened up about some concerns with his marriage and fears about his job. Then, he began to inquire about Phil's faith. "You're not like some of the 'Born Again' I know at work," he said. Brett was drawn to the stability Phil's faith gave him. He saw how Phil's beliefs played out consistently in his marriage, on the job, and even with his taxes. A bridge of trust and friendship was being built. Then, one Saturday, as they mounted their bikes to head home, Brett said, "You know Phil, I want what you have." He accepted an invitation to church, then a men's small group, and a few weeks later, Brett was baptized into Christ.

When we think of reaching people with the Good News of Jesus, we tend to think of how to talk about it. Evangelism is pictured as cornering someone in an airport, shoving a tract in someone's hand, or going door-to-door with a rehearsed speech. Some even speak of "winning" the loss to Jesus, which makes it sound like those who don't know Christ are our opponents in a war, who eventually succumb to our torturous techniques and are talked into agreeing with our point of view about God. But as this story reminds us, it is often not our words but our whole life that speaks the loudest message. Paul says,

"Be wise in the way you act toward outsiders; make the most of every opportunity." Colossians 4:5

God wants to use us to reach those whose hearts are far away from God's heart. Be aware that everything you say and do is a witness of one kind or another. Words about Christ don't have much power when they come from a person who doesn't represent Him well. We are not called to impress people but to influence them. And the most influential tool in the world is a Christ-like life. Francis of Assisi said, "Preach the gospel always—if necessary, use words." Nothing you say will overcome how you live.

When Christians fail to live up to the character of Christ, we lose our voice. Some have written off Christ because Jesus' ambassadors haven't always represented Him very well. Even if they got the words right, their actions spoke so loudly that they drowned out the message. We are called to preach the Good News with our lives...and, if necessary, use words. Peter writes a letter to Christians who lived in a world largely hostile to their beliefs. They knew they were not at home in the world, and they always faced the potential of serious persecution. To help them know how to live in a society that was so antagonistic to their faith, Peter gives them some remarkable counsel.

What an amazing strategy for facing a culture that is opposed to the Gospel. Confrontation occurs, not in the words of the church but in the dramatic contrast between the lives of those who follow Christ and those who do not. Peter knows that Christians successfully "argue" for the merit of God's will simply by living it out. Displaying the Ten Commandments in the courthouse might be a useful reminder, but displaying the Sermon on the Mount in the life of every Christ follower would change the planet and draw the world to Christ. When we finally "live such good lives" (1 Peter 2:12), you will hear someone say, "I want what you have."

Questions:

1. What do you think of people who speak the Word but fail to show it in the way they live?

2. What Christ-like quality would be most attractive to someone you know and would like to invite to church?

3. What a powerful text. It starts out a little harsh, doesn't it? Is Paul saying that all these people are unwelcome in the church?

STUDY 7 – GIVE

Study 1 – Generosity
Read: Matthew 6:19-21

"But since you excel in everything—in faith, in speech, in knowledge, in complete earnestness [and in your love for us]—see that you also excel in this grace of giving."
2 Corinthians 8:7

A life following after Christ is a life of generosity. In Scripture, we are repeatedly taught that God gives to us so that we can excel in giving to others. Like rivers in which the life-giving rain flows throughout the land, God wants us to receive good blessings and share them with others. By surrendering everything to Christ, we are enabled to hold our possessions loosely and give up our financial resources.

Our world tempts us with the comforts of wealth and leisure, frightens us with images of poverty and want, and tricks us into believing that with enough money, we can be secure and find contentment in material things. We are easily fooled. But God says, "I am the source of your life and will supply your needs." As with so many of His teachings, we can learn to give when we learn to trust God.

In the reading today, Jesus said that your heart (i.e., your love and devotion, affection and concern) follows your money. This lesson offers the opportunity to examine your heart by examining your financial habits. The challenge this week is to imagine you are a visitor from a foreign land who understands this heart principle that Jesus taught. Investigate what you value, how you spend your money, and where you put your priorities. Take an honest look at the things you want. Ask yourself, are these the things that really matter in life? Are they faithful to me, and can I rely on them, or are they false loves and lusts?

Most of what I spend is money that I owe. I am under obligation. The money that I "give" to my mortgage company is really a repayment of the debt I incurred upon the purchase of my house. When I pay my electric bill, I am paying for electricity that I have already used. We're always paying or repaying for the things we need and the things we use. There is little that is "donated" rather than spent in exchange for goods or services.

God is unlike this in every way. God doesn't owe anything to anyone. God is entirely self-sufficient. Anything that comes from God is provided as a true gift. From the time of creation, God continues to give with abundance beyond our imagination. God gives life and existence, hope, and peace. It is from Him we receive the ability to work and the joy of rest. All are gifts from God.

We have seen in the past few weeks that all these steps to which God calls us flow out of the very character of our Creator. Giving is no exception. God relates to the creation as the Ultimate Giver. Humans may twist and destroy these things, turning them into evil, but God's giving is plentiful in its general abundance and specific in its providential care.

The Psalmist sings,

"The LORD is trustworthy in all he promises and faithful in all he does. The LORD upholds all who fall and lifts up all who are bowed down. The eyes of all look to you, and you give them their food at the proper time. You open your hand and satisfy the desires of every living thing." Psalm 145:13b -16.

God promises to give blessings to those who live in obedience to His Word gives salvation through the sacrifice of His precious Son, Jesus Christ. Beyond a doubt, this truth is the most significant and dramatic demonstration of God's nature as a giver that we will ever experience.

Questions:

1. How do you explain "even our 'hard-earned money' is the result of God's gift?"

2. How does your attitude toward your possessions need to change?

3. How does this affect your attitude of giving?

4. How do you feel about the statement "fully surrendering our hearts to Christ?"

5. Can you fully surrender to Christ and still hold on to an attitude of selfishness?

Study 2 - Heart Check
Read: Acts 4:32–37

> *"Joseph, a Levite from Cyprus, whom the apostles called*
> *Barnabas (which means son of encouragement), sold a field he*
> *owned and brought the money and put it at the apostles' feet."*
> *(vs. 36–37)*

What a radical practice of generosity! A ministry team purchases a wheelchair lift for the van of a team member with a special needs son. A small group provides child care, meals, and house cleaning for a pregnant woman caring for her dying mother. A family in need of a minivan is given one by another family in the church. Groceries are provided to those in need of food, and clothing is provided to those in need of clothes. Computers, vehicles, tools, and money are all shared when needs become apparent. These real-life contemporary examples sound a lot like the first-century church Paul describes in the reading for today.

Many contemporary churches talk about giving exclusively as a function of gratitude to God or obedience to God's commands. Certainly, both of these are valid and Scriptural reasons for giving. However, it is interesting to notice that the motivation for giving that Luke describes is not doctrinal or moral, but relational. The people in Acts are not giving because it is right or good but because those around them are in need. Like Jesus, they cared for one another with compassion. Notice the first sentence. "All the believers were one in heart and mind." The basis for the radical lifestyle of giving is not hatred of wealth but love for a neighbor. It isn't that they didn't care about their possessions; it is simply that they cared more about each other. This new church is sharing life together. As a result, they share wealth out of love for each other and knowledge of each other's situation.

It is also important to recognize that this is not an act of Christian socialism. The Bible does not describe a mandate to help others. There was a system for distributing goods to those in need, but there was no system for soliciting donations. Then, as now, Christian giving begins in the heart of the giver and not in the demand of the institution. This kind of committed sharing is still expected of the church. It should still characterize the Christian community. To achieve such a lifestyle, the church must recommit to three patterns. Most basically, the church must commit to living life together. As American culture becomes increasingly isolated, we will likely know more about the lives of strangers, such as celebrities, than the lives of our neighbors and perhaps even our families. Americans drive into their garages or lock the doors on their apartments, never meet their neighbors, and have only sporadic and trivial contact with friends. Given this culture of isolation, Christians must intentionally build communities of intimacy and interdependency. People cannot share with those whom they do not trust, and they cannot trust those whom they do not know.

Secondly, we must understand the kind of unity to which God has called the church. Paul describes the church as a body. In a body, the parts are so intimately joined that all know experiences of pain and pleasure. Certainly, Christians ought to live life together, but the Scripture is clear that the church is one body even when it does not live up to its unity. Christians need to claim this belief. The world is consistent in teaching that we are isolated individuals and should look out for ourselves and perhaps our families. The church must be similarly consistent by teaching the opposite. God tells us that we are not self-sufficient; rather, we are one.

Having changed the pattern of our actions, we must change the pattern of the heart. We have been trained never to give what we might someday need. Furthermore, we have been even better trained never to accept the gifts of another. We must un-train ourselves. God expects that churches will be the kind of place where no one would think to keep extra for themselves when a brother or sister in Christ is hungry or homeless. Similarly, the notion that a Christian might refuse the gift of another denies God's proclamation that the church is one body, one family, and one people. Christians so flippantly say they won't take charity, forgetting that to make such a claim is to reject the very center of the Gospel.

Questions:

1. When you give, do you think more about gratitude and obedience to God or helping meet the spiritual and tangible needs of others?

2. How do these motives work together to improve our giving?

3. In what way is a Christian giving voluntarily? In what way is a Christian giving expected?

4. How does giving help overcome society's trend toward isolation?

5. How does accepting gifts from others make you feel?

Day 3 - Beyond Human Understanding
Read: Acts 15:36-41

A friend of mine had her life changed when she encountered someone who gave, like Jesus. It wasn't really one thing in particular that he did, but rather just the way that he lived his life. He always had a word of encouragement for someone who was having a tough day. If he met someone on the street who needed food, he would take him to dinner first and then to the store so they had provisions for the week to follow. He was always willing to lend out his books, his CDs, and his car. And once, when he earned an extra hundred dollars from a side job, he simply handed it to my friend, sensing she needed it more than he did. This kind of generosity can be hard for me to imagine. This is a life that is so different than what I know. I am tempted to soothe myself by saying that it can't be done.

Now, of course, this isn't true; God would not ask me to do what I cannot do, so the fact that God asks is proof enough that it is possible. My friend's story is proof that it is possible. Yet my imagination is hindered by the more commonplace realities that I have seen. Furthermore, I fail to dream about all the giving possibilities and I am tempted to settle for merely being more generous than my neighbor. Thankfully, God has given us models of people just like you and me who live out this giving principle. Let's take a look at such an example.

In the book of Acts, we encounter the ministry of a man called Barnabas. His needs and desires were not any different than mine. He was not God or Jesus. He was not perfect, yet he managed a lifestyle of generosity that inspired others. We meet Barnabas in the fourth chapter of Acts. He is the man who sells a field and gives the proceeds to the church. He is the poster child the caring community that had developed in Jerusalem. In this introduction to him, we learn that he is living in such a way that he knows the needs of his fellow Christians. When he feels their needs, he responds. He has extra, more than he needs. What a concept! His heart is configured in such a way that he asks himself, "How can I allow myself to have extra when someone in the family of God does not have enough?"

We also learn that not only is he a giver of money, but he is also a giver of encouragement. His given name was Joseph, but we know him as Barnabas (son of encouragement). What kind of life he must have lived to receive such a wonderful name. To give bread to others is good, but to give bread and hope is godly. Barnabas' giving continues to grow as his story progresses. After Paul's conversion, he returns to Jerusalem where he is greeted by great distrust. It is Barnabas who gives Paul an opportunity to enter the congregation and join the fellowship. This gift of welcome and inclusion begins Paul's transition from feared outsider to leader in the church.

Later, a need for leadership arises in the Antioch church. It had a huge Gentile population and was filled with new Christians with no religious background. Few in the church had been raised in Judaism, so they knew little about God's character, grace, and morality. It is not surprising that the Jerusalem church sent Barnabas to assist with the leadership of the church. As the "son of encouragement," he understands the complexities of this culturally diverse church and is open to including those who were former enemies of the church.

In his Antioch ministry, he gives a second great gift to Paul - his first major ministry opportunity. Up to this point, Paul has met with trouble in his ministries. However, the church in Antioch is the perfect fit for him. There is not a large Jewish population, so Paul will have few old enemies, and the congregation is hungry to learn about the God they have begun to serve.

Paul and Barnabas eventually part company when Barnabas wants to give the young John Mark, who had left their first mission journey, a second chance at the ministry. However, at a later time Paul would come to depend upon the seasoned and diligent John Mark, to whom Barnabas had given a second chance and trained on the mission field.

Barnabas lived his life in a posture of giving. At all times, he assessed the needs of others and the blessings that God had given him. When his gifts were not enough, he brought others alongside and taught

them the art of giving. Two thousand years later this "son of encouragement" is an example for all of us to live our lives with open hands.

Questions:

1. Is it helpful for you to see that giving and generosity are not really about having lots of money?

2. The example of Barnabas shows us that radical giving is always on the lookout for needs it can meet. How could you live on the lookout for others in need?

3. How can you help and support the needs of those around you?

4. What are some ways you can give to others without giving physical things like money or gifts?

Day 4 - It's not Yours to Keep
Read: Mark 12: 41-44

I remember my first sleepless night that was inspired by guilt. My family stopped for gas on the way home from somewhere. We rarely indulged whims, but for some reason, I asked to go in and get some beef jerky. My dad gave me twenty dollars. I never expected he would say yes to such a silly desire. I was so thankful. I went in and bought a piece. When I returned, he forgot to ask for the change. I didn't offer it. The money stayed in my jeans pocket.

It was a long night. At first, I lay awake wondering what to do with the money. I was young enough and that twenty dollars was a lot of money. As the night wore on, my thoughts changed. I remembered that it wasn't my money; it was my father's money. He meant to give me beef jerky; that alone was a special treat. For me to keep the rest was theft, and it was theft from my dad. Worse, it was theft from my dad when he was being extra nice to me. The next morning, when I saw him, I breezily said, "Hey, Dad, I forgot to give you the change from last night." It was a lie. I did not forget.

When I consider Christian generosity, I usually wonder, "How much should I give?" I assume that I possess all this money that I have earned, and I wonder what portion I should give away. But that is not the case. All that we have belongs to God, and we are just the managers. The question that Christians should ask regarding their finances is not,

"How much of my money should I give?" Rather, we ask, "How much of God's money should I keep?" Those seeking to follow Christ must learn to hold their money and possessions very loosely.

The walk of following Jesus is a walk in a foreign land. The true home of a Christian is not earth but heaven. The resources that God has placed in our hands are intended to be traveling money. These are not, however, the travels of a tourist. Christians are not journeying through the world to see the sights and enjoy the luxurious accommodations; our resources are not designed to help us collect souvenirs. Rather, we are called to be pilgrims and sojourners. Anything God gives us is to provide for our journey and to enable us to help others we meet along the path. This understanding creates a whole new set of questions as

Christians approach their wealth. What is the source of my security? Does my use of my money support my journey after Christ or distract me from it? What about my car? My gadgets? How can I invest God's money to serve the journey of others? Paul reminds Timothy,

"For we brought nothing into the world, and we can take nothing out of it. But if we have food and clothing, we will be content with that. Those who want to get rich fall into temptation and a trap and into many foolish and harmful desires that plunge people into ruin and destruction. For the love of money is a root of all kinds of evil. Some people, eager for money, have wandered from the faith and pierced themselves with many griefs." 1 Timothy 6:7–10

"If we have food and clothing, we will be content with that." Those are the words of a pilgrim, of someone who holds life's possessions loosely so that they might be used in God's service. God gives wealth, and like all of God's gifts, it can be used to serve the walk after Christ, or it can be used to impede it. The wealth that God has given to you is for your food and shelter. God wants you to buy those things that you need. But God has not invited us to keep the change. That money in my jeans pocket that night was stolen from my father, though he never knew it. God wants you to hold loosely to the wealth God has given you. Know that God has put it in your hands so that it might serve God's purposes and not only your own.

In Mark 12:41–44, Jesus identifies an unlikely hero. He describes the scene outside the temple with people parading by, plunking large coins in the trumpet-like receptacles. Then, a small, elderly woman deposits a penny. How is it that Jesus could say she put more in than all the others? What did He mean?

Questions:

1. Why is the widow the hero of this story?

2. What does "not equal giving but equal sacrifice" mean to you?

3. Are you tempted to hoard God's money for your own purposes?

4. How might you begin to loosen your grip on your finances?

5. How do you feel about people who are generous?

Day 5 – Structured Giving
Read: Acts 5:1-11

Just making a commitment to hold your possessions loosely is not enough. If we are honest with ourselves, we know that this commitment will be forgotten as quickly as last year's resolution to lose 20 pounds. Unless, in addition to your resolution, you make a plan, and you carry it out. When I just state my desire to take up some new practice but don't make a plan, it is an insincere desire that never happens. So, if you have accepted Christ's call to hold your possessions loosely and give generously, you need to ask, "How and to what will I give?" Broadly, the answer is that we should give with discipline but not under compulsion. Christians must continually remind one another that they are freed from any legalistic burdens regarding giving.

Our common human pattern is to turn "oughts" into "musts" and begin to use our man-made laws to regulate our neighbors. This is the opposite of Christian giving. Giving done to meet some human rule is taxation and not at all what God desires. In one of the most dramatic stories of the New Testament, we see the tragic consequences of a legalistic understanding of giving. Ananias and Sapphira were Christians living in Jerusalem in the first century. Many in the church were selling property and other valued assets and giving the proceeds to the church for the care of the poor. Ananias and Sapphira sold some land and gave some of the money to the church but bragged about having given it all.

Look at Peter's explanation:

"Ananias, how is it that Satan has so filled your heart that you have lied to the Holy Spirit and have kept for yourself some of the money you received for the land? Didn't it belong to you before it was sold? And after it was sold, wasn't the money at your disposal? What made you think of doing such a thing? You have not lied just to men but to God."

Luke described this community in Acts 4:32,

"No one claimed that any of his possessions was his own, but they shared everything they had."

Christian giving grows out of a heart of gratitude and a desire to participate in the purposes of God. Then, as now, so much that God wants to do in the world costs money. To send missionaries, as the Church at Antioch sent Paul and Barnabas, required many people to partner with God financially. To secure facilities costs money in every age and these needs are no less important to God's purpose because they are mundane.

Unfortunately, in order to avoid legalistic giving, many Christians are resistant to any attempt to provide discipline and structure in their giving. Those who would resist all structure might encourage Christians to simply give as they feel led or when the opportunity presents itself. Certainly, to give in such situations is appropriate but to limit our giving to such situations is foolish and cuts us off from the kind of joys that come from disciplined giving.

Paul suggests to the church in Corinth,

"Now about the collection for the Lord's people: Do what I told the Galatian churches to do. On the first day of every week, each one of you should set aside a sum of money in keeping with his income, saving it up, so that when I come no collections will have to be made." 1 Corinthians 16:1, 2

The principle here is straightforward. If we intend to have our financial actions meet our financial intentions, we must give the money away first. The advice to set the money aside reflects the reality of our habits. If you wait to consider how much to give when sitting in a church building on Sunday morning, likely the money will be spent or spoken for, or unavailable. In contrast, if you plan for giving, and give before any other money is spent, you find great freedom because you do not need to wrestle with the decision of what to give each Sunday.

For many Christians, one such plan for giving is the tithe (10%). Freed from the law, that tithe can be an inspiring and challenging benchmark to begin to give to God. For some who are financially hard-pressed, this mark should not be an oppressive burden or a legalistic requirement for faithfulness (although it is amazing what happens when we desire to give generously and trust God to provide). For many American Christians, even this benchmark is holding on to much more than is needed for the journey. The center of the matter is this: choose to give out of love; plan to give with commitment; then give as you have decided.

Questions:

1. Is your Christian giving systematic or spontaneous? What are the advantages of each?

2. How might giving, even when you don't feel like it, eventually change your feelings about giving?

3. What things do you desire that keep you from giving to others?

Additional Reading: 2 Corinthians 8:7.

Day 6 - How Much?
Read: 2 Corinthians 9:6–11

I remember learning a game once at a college retreat. The night was late, and the crowd was mellow. Only one person knew the game, and she was excited to teach it to us. Many were tired, including me, and so we expressed some wariness. I was in charge of the event and was especially concerned, as I did not want to wear everyone out and end the evening on a down note. I had little confidence in a strange game working this late at night. She pleaded, "Just go with it; it is great." She began to explain the rules, and my worries rose. The rules were weird, and they didn't seem to make up a game. They were clear enough to understand; it was just that they didn't add up to a game. She replied, "Just go with it; it is great. Trust me, if anyone else here had played, they would agree with me." Of course, no one else had. And that was part of my worry. We were an experienced and diverse group of college students from student ministries all over the country. If this game was so great, surely one of us would have heard of it. I started to call it off before we even started. I didn't want everyone to hate the game and perhaps she would think of more rules if we let her sleep on it. She pleaded, "Just give it a chance." I relented.

Three or four hours later, with my ribs and jaw aching from laughing and my voice hoarse from cheering, we reluctantly conceded that we must go to bed. I stayed up a few minutes after everyone else to consider how we might squeeze in a few more hours of the couch game into our retreat.

This is a little bit of how the miracle of Christian giving works. The rules are disarming in their simplicity. God and Christ give us a torrent of blessing and grace and forgiveness and life that never stops unless we refuse, and even then, we are given so much more than we know. God calls us to be agents of generosity and grace to one another and to the world. As the Apple Computer advertisements used to say, "There is no step three." Unfortunately, so few have played the game that it is hard to find many to give testimony. Those few who have tried sound like my friend who had trouble convincing us to play her game, "Just give it a shot; it will bring such joy to your life." The human race is so fearful. We believe that there is only so much wealth and blessing and joy to go around, and we are afraid that if we give ours away, we will be left empty. Nothing could be further from the truth. We try to be ponds, holding in the rain God sends on all people. God wants us to be laughing brooks, singing streams and roaring rivers; receiving God's blessing and letting it flow through us to all people.

One of the most amazing and consistent realities of Scripture is that God never blesses someone for their own gain. God blessed Abraham so that Abraham might be a blessing to all nations. God preserved and promoted Joseph so that Joseph might save the lives of his dishonest brothers. God led, punished, and restored Israel so that other nations might be drawn to God. God blessed the apostles so that all may believe. God empowers individuals with spiritual gifts for the good of the church.

In these few verses are the surprisingly simple principles of Christian giving. God blesses us not for our good but so that we can participate in blessing others. How remarkable, how wonderful, how amazing. It is as if God says to all, "Become a river; trust that I will give you what you must have for this journey, and let my blessings flow through you to all others. Then trust that the heavens will open and my blessing will pour out not just in wealth but in every way so that you have a part in the joy of blessing others."

Questions:

1. Has anyone ever tried to persuade you about the joy and blessing of Christian giving?

2. Who could you ask about his or her experiences with Christian generosity?

3. In what way do Christians sometimes turn God's promise of blessing into something selfish?

4. For you, what is the most exciting reward of Christian giving?

Day 7 - Practical Giving
Read: Ecclesiastes 2:4-11

In the next study we are going to look at the subject of service. However, as we give of our resources it isn't just about money, but also how much we give of ourselves. It isn't enough to give money. In fact, in family relationships giving of self is far more important than money. We all have a finite amount of time on this earth. We each have 24 hours a day, seven days each week and 52 weeks each year, should we not die in the meantime. It is much easier for most of us to give a few dollars instead of interrupting our own priorities and taking time for others.

I worked for a small company in Lancaster, Pennsylvania. The company president called us together for a company meeting. At the end of the meeting he announced that his wife was leaving him because he spent too much time at the workplace. He explained that she was making a stupid mistake because he was spending the time to build the business so that she and the children would have all the things they wanted. It was his opinion that she would eventually regret leaving him and all he had to offer.

This is a very typical reaction on both sides of the marriage partnership. She can't have enough of his time so she ditches him only to get none of his time. He thinks that things are more important than relationships and continues to focus his attention on the business instead of the family. The children will grow up feeling abandoned and even useless. It is no wonder they suffer from depression or even result to senseless acts of violence to vent their anger and frustration.

I don't recall that anybody on their death bed ever said, "I wish I had spent more time at the office." It is as important that we manage our time as it is our money. So how can we give of ourselves in ways other than money? We can start by volunteer work. The easiest way to get involved is in the church. There is always a place to help out, teaching Sunday school, driving the church bus, setting up chairs or helping in the office. The list is endless. It even extends to visiting those who are shut in or serving meals to invalids. People volunteer to work in hospitals or in nursing homes. It doesn't always require special skills. Just listening can be a valuable service.

When you donate clothing to the Salvation Army it is done from a distance. A more personal way to give is by sharing your house with someone in need. This can be a room for an exchange student or temporary living space for a visiting missionary. Maybe you can go even further and provide a permanent place to live for someone in need. Some people are able to donate blood to preserve the lives of others. The Bible says that life is in the blood and this is abundantly clear through blood donations. When you give of yourself you will find that you receive back more than you give out.

Throughout this study of giving we have focused on your generosity by giving time, money and resources. Giving through churches and philanthropic organizations ideally remove the giver from the emotional exchanges between individuals, but this isn't always the case. Sometimes the giving is directly to meet some immediate need. It can be troublesome when giving money to another or by sharing your home with them. These situations can lead to serious consequences. The receiver can become dependent on you or even come to expect your giving. They can become resentful that you have more than they have. In some cases, especially in jail, the receiver may see you as an easy touch and take advantage of you, so you must be careful about to whom and how you give. A request for money is the first sign of danger.

If you loan money with a promise of repayment a contract must be written that explains the agreed upon terms in order to prevent any misunderstanding. If you share your home with them on a temporary basis this also should be documented, especially to include the length of their stay.

Questions and activities:

1. Can you remember a time where you used money to avoid giving your time?

2. In what ways have you been able to give to others without giving money?

3. Make a list of some ways that you can begin giving even more of your time.

4. Have you had a parent that didn't spend their time with you? How did it make you feel?

5. If you have a spouse, children or other family member, make a list of ways you could give to them using your time.

STUDY 8 – SERVE

Day 1- Being Involved
Read: Ephesians 2:1-10

It was November, which meant that with a few exceptions, most of my small town was focused on football. I was one of those few exceptions. I went to all the games because I was in the band, but I was there for the fun and the music, not the game.

Another one of those exceptions was the high school boys' basketball coach. He was focused on preseason practices and grades. In particular, he knew that his two-star players for the upcoming season were both failing math. If they had a D or below by the end of the semester, they could not play for the last half of the season, which of course was the half that really mattered. I was a senior, but since I had no athletic skills to speak of and little interest in basketball, I had never met the coach. So, I was more than a bit surprised to be called out of class one day and directed to report to the office of the basketball coach.

He introduced himself and the two tall sophomores sitting in his office. He told me that he needed me to help out the team. I almost laughed. He explained that these guys needed a tutor who could help them to become C students by the end of the semester. I took the job. To this day, it was the oddest tutoring job I ever had. We met a few mornings each week and often in the afternoons. I gave extra homework and we went back and covered a lot of material. At first, they resisted. Neither was there by choice. A few days into the experience the coach stopped me again and asked if they were working hard. They weren't, so I told him. I found out later that for two days they were not allowed to practice, but rather had to sit in the bleachers working math problems. After that, they were the best students I ever taught.

When the season began, a curious thing happened. I had to be at the opening game with the band. For the first time, I actually paid attention to the game. I knew two of the players now. It was pretty clear why the coach cared enough to work them so hard. They were good. I started to cheer. My friends wondered what I was doing. For those two players I don't think their experience with me left a lasting impression. They worked hard for nine weeks, did all their homework, got B's and even a couple of A's on quizzes and tests, and ended the semester with C's. That secured their eligibility and they immediately quit the tutoring. But for me it changed that whole basketball season. I was a part of the team now (even if I was the part that would never be acknowledged over the loudspeaker or with a jersey). It was one of the most rewarding tutoring jobs I ever held. What I had to offer was needed and I gave it, and we had a great season.

Long after they had quit studying and gone back to failing math, I could watch their effortless play and know that I had contributed to their victory. That is the joy of serving. When we serve we do one of the very things for which God has saved us. We so often talk about all the things from which God has saved us. But there are many things that God has saved us for, and one of those is service. The second chapter of Ephesians teaches us that we have been saved from death. We have been saved by grace. We have been saved through faith. We have been saved for good works that God has prepared for us to do.

When we serve, we join with Christ in His purposes, and Christ promises that when we serve we are serving Him (Matthew 25:40). Just as I never valued basketball until I gave my service to the game, we can never find joy in this world while all we do is take what we can get.

Rather we find real joy when we live in the way God created us to live. God has created us for service.

Questions:

1. Have you ever found yourself enjoying something more because you worked to make it happen?

2. Why are we tempted to focus more on what we are saved from, than what we are saved for?

3. In what area of your life do you need to begin to experience the joy of serving?

Day 2 – Power
Read: Philippians 2:5-11

Most of us learned how power works very early in life. We learned that those with power rule; those without power serve. On the playground power was size and the biggest kid made the rules. In our economy money is power. Those who need money do what they are told, and those who have it tell others what to do. I have heard this stated as the modern Golden Rule: "He with the gold, rules."

Usually we don't question this principle. We accept that the weak serve the strong. It likely never occurred to you that it could be any other way. Most of us find ourselves somewhere in the middle. Much of our day is spent reporting to someone in authority, and the other part of the day is spent making the rules for our subordinates. For some of us it may be the rules for our dog. We rarely question this arrangement because our culture has taught us that this dynamic of master and servant is just how the world works. Those with power and money use it to control those without.

God is not in the middle; He is Lord. Consequently, if the world is supposed to work the way we have been taught, one might suspect that God serves no one. As the top authority with all the power, everyone would be made to serve God. But that is not the way things work in the Kingdom of God. No one is ever made to serve God. God does not "lord it over creation" even though God is "Lord of Creation." In fact, God helps and serves creation. Over and over again, God's people acknowledge that God is their helper. Psalm after Psalm proclaims that God has served. They do not try to explain the paradox; they simply give praise for the help that God has brought. (Check out Psalm 33, 70, 115, 121,124, and 146 for examples.)

The term "helper" used to describe God in these psalms is also the same term used to describe Eve. God looks for a helper for Adam and therefore creates Eve (Genesis 2:18). As a culture, we have bought into the lie that service is tied to subordination. As a result, we sometimes read the description of Eve as a helper designed for

Adam and think that this means she is his subordinate. This is a gross misunderstanding, for this word translated "helper" is most often used to describe God's relationship with humans. One would be foolish to argue that God is our subordinate. Rather, God demonstrates that to serve another is a position of great honor.

We see in Mark 10:42–45 the teaching of Jesus,

> *"You know that those who are regarded as rulers of the Gentiles lord it over them, and their high officials exercise authority over them. Not so with you. Instead, whoever wants to become great among you must be your servant, and whoever wants to be first must be slave of all. For even the Son of Man did not come to be served, but to serve, and to give his life as a ransom for many."*

This truth was clearly understood by George Washington Carver in his favorite saying:

> *"It is not the style of clothes one wears, neither the kind of automobile one drives, nor the amount of money one has in the bank, that counts. These mean nothing. It is simply service that measures success."*

Questions:

1. How does the church sometimes accept the world's notion of power and authority?

2. How have you seen God rule through service rather than through power and dominion?

3. In what area of your life do you need to wait in hope for the Lord who is your "help and shield"?

4. How do you measure success?

5. When have you tried to lord it over somebody else? How did that work for you?

Day 3 – ServeFest
Read: Micah 6:6–8

In Study 5 about Growth, we explored the idea of whole-life worship being more than just attending church on Sunday. In this study of Serving we look at another way to worship. The Israelites were taught to make animal sacrifices to God and offerings of oils and grain. They were required to dedicate their first-born children to the Lord at the Temple. But none of these sacrificial rituals were any good if they did not act justly, show mercy to others and humble themselves.

It is part of our Christian identity to worship God by pronouncing glory, honor and praise on His Holy Name. But words can easily substitute for the true acts of worship demonstrated by serving the needs of others. In fact, it is a steady refrain in Scripture that our worship, as normally understood, only makes sense when we are partners with God in serving the outcast, the orphan, the widow, and all those who are least in our society. We are to be the people committed to the needs of the least and the lost of society. James 1:27 teaches what we have already heard from the prophets,

> *"Religion that God our Father accepts as pure and faultless is this: to look after orphans and widows in their distress and to keep oneself from being polluted by the world."*

A few years ago, a church in our community began a project called "ServeFest." Each year, a day is set aside to demonstrate Christ's love by being Jesus' hands and feet to the community. Hundreds of volunteers join together into teams that fan out in all directions. They paint, clean up trash, cut lawns, remove weeds and make repairs for playgrounds, school buildings, civic groups, and other community service organizations. Over the years a number of other churches have joined-in spreading the idea into communities and cities as far as 35 miles away.

The ServeFest concept has been further expanded by the church. A church staff member organizes service opportunities to help the elderly and infirm with fix-up projects around their homes. Each month on the "Second Saturday Service Day" volunteers team up to go fourth to serve these human needs. Besides showing mercy to others and the love of God to the community, individuals are given the opportunity to serve Christ, working together, and learning the joy of serving others. This is a true act of worship.

Questions and activities:

1. What does it mean to you to be merciful?

2. In what ways have you been guilty of pride?

3. Do you think an angry person can demonstrate God's love?

4. How does this study change your attitude toward service?

5. Make a list of ways that you can serve God and discuss them with your mentor.

Day 4 – Mutual Support
Read: Romans 16

Whenever I attend an event that involves a celebrity I get an uncomfortable feeling. If I am at a concert or a lecture series, I always feel a little uncomfortable at all the attention given to the star or the main speaker. At a concert, it is the star's face on the T-shirts and CDs at the sales table. At a lecture, the writer's face is on the books. Even at Christian events where I enjoy the artist and respect the speaker I have this sense of discomfort. I probably feel it the most if I happen to show up early to see that the room is empty of fans but filled with workers preparing for the event. Often, dozens of people dressed in black clothes so they will not be seen, are working to prepare for the event. Many of these people have traveled or worked overtime to support this event. They don't write songs or books, so they won't have tables selling themselves.

I sometimes feel this same discomfort as I study the early church as well. We can learn a lot about Paul from Scripture, but those working behind the scenes to help him seem unnoticed. We know a bit about Timothy, but very little about his mother and grandmother. In Paul's second letter to Timothy (2 Tim. 1:5) Paul writes,

"I am reminded of your sincere faith, which first lived in your grandmother Lois and in your mother Eunice, and I am persuaded now lives in you also."

What an intriguing statement! These were devout women and must have been early converts. What were their lives like? Did they work with Paul in those early years?

It is because of this discomfort that I like Romans 16. Paul was planning to go to Rome to establish a mission base to Spain, and he wants to let the church know that he is coming. Paul was a celebrity in the world of the early church. His mission successes were well known, and the churches were already passing around his letters. But Paul recognizes that his ministry worked only because of many others who have contributed to him. So in the sixteenth chapter, Paul takes the opportunity to mention those in the church who have supported him in his ministry.

Isn't that an amazing list? You may not have heard of any of these people, yet their ministry laid the foundation for the work of Paul. They shared his jail cell and served with him as apostles. I wonder what Mary did. Did she cook, or open her home? Think about Rufus' mother. What did Paul need that day (or week or month)? When did Rufus' mother become like a mother to him? Did she give him a warm meal, a hug, or a shoulder to cry on? Perhaps she packed his bags with food for his journey or visited him in prison.

Even Jesus found his ministry supported by the people around him. He was fed by the generosity of strangers and friends. He stayed in others' homes and relied upon their care for him. You may sometimes feel that the acts of service given to you or the acts of service you perform don't matter. You may be tempted to resent those whose service leads to praise or fame or shy away from thanks given to you for your help. In those moments remember that Christ calls all of us to work together for an eternal purpose. Remember Romans 16. Each one of these people mattered in the ministry of Paul. And in our world today, our acts of service matter. Serve and be served with a joyful heart.

Questions:

1. What would happen at a concert if only the stars and the fans showed up, but the nameless crew did not?

2. Who would put you on their list of helper, encourager or supporter?

3. How might you support the work and witness of someone else?

4. Is a person who is critical of others a supporter or detractor?

Day 5 – Gifts
Read: 1 Corinthians 12:1–11

I am a very organized person. These organizational patterns are visible in the way I draw, in how I write and the way I conduct my daily schedule. This is a natural gift that is just part of my genetic code and early childhood. What little creativity I have is shown in mechanical ideas and inventions. In grade school I drew a fire truck and showed it to have steel bands inside the tires to prevent punctures causing flat tires. I even suggested to my father that automobiles should have brakes on all four wheels so they could stop faster. Little did I know this was already the way they were made. Maybe the steel bands in the fire truck tires was somewhat close to steel belted radials, but way ahead of their eventual development.

Our natural gifts are not the same as the gifts mentioned in today's reading. Although our natural abilities are an important part of serving God, these spiritual gifts are those provided by God to meet specific needs as we are called to serve in His kingdom. God poured out special gifts upon composers and artists during the age of enlightenment to give us the classical compositions of Johann Sebastian Bach, Wolfgang Amadeus Mozart, and George Frideric Handel. Handel completed the *Messiah* in 24 days, sometimes going without eating. He is said to have "seen the face of God" while working on this majestic composition. Mozart was composing music at the age of five. His complex symphonies were composed without any corrections to the musical score!

Notice in Matthew 10 how God gives gifts to the disciples as He sends them out to preach the Good News. God continues to provide us with the gifts we need to do his will. Most Biblical scholars are inclined to restrict the gifts to the 22 or so mentioned in the New Testament. Are we to assume that this list of gifts is complete, that God has no other gifts to give? Gifts are also mentioned in Exodus 28:3. Here God gives wisdom to artisans for creating items of beauty. Some people have been gifted with the power of intercessory prayer, but prayer is not one of those on the list. What we can be sure about is that God has given, or will give the gifts necessary for us to carry out His purpose in our lives. He has said not to fear about what we are to say, as the Holy Spirit will provide the correct words when they are needed. God does not ask us to serve without equipping us. He will provide for our needs as we seek to follow His will in serving others.

I Corinthians 12 is the introduction to three chapters on the nature of Spiritual Gifts and the dangers of considering that some gifts are more important than others. The Corinthians had come to believe that some were gifted and others were not. Some were bragging that they had the more important gift. Paul rejects this idea. First of all, notice that God has empowered all Christians for service. All have been gifted. Second, notice that the source of all gifts is the same. Third, there is one reason that God gives us these gifts: so that we can serve the common good.

No gift that comes from God was meant to build up the recipient. God gives to you so that you might bless others. You are gifted. God has placed in your life the skills, the time and the resources that God wants to give through you to others. Don't let these precious gifts become useless stuff.

Questions:

1. In what ways has your life affected others for either good or bad?

2. Have you ever thought about your gifts and abilities as being God given?

3. What natural abilities have you been given?

4. Pray to discover your spiritual abilities and list some way you can use them to serve others.

Further Reading: 1 Peter 4:8-11

Day 6 – Redeeming the Time
Read: Ephesians 5:15-20

God had been very generous and provided a big house in a beautiful setting on one acre, more or less. In the yard we had many tees and shrubs, even a fishpond. All of this backed up to the State Forest. We had a woodstove that was used for much of the winter heat. I found that much of my free time was spent taking care of this wonderful property, cleaning the pond, feeding the goldfish, mowing the grass, raking the leaves, cutting firewood, moving firewood, and trimming the many trees and shrubs. I was forced to say "no" when asked to help somebody else or to take on more ministry responsibilities at church. I had to find a way to prioritize my activities and free up some time. I finally reached a point where I had to say "goodbye" to this place called home for some 25 years and move into a house where the property was small and the outside work was in the hands of the neighborhood association.

I think that one of the reasons many people attend church every week and leave there relatively unchanged is that, when they arrive, the week ahead is already full. Imagine that the songs or the Scripture or the sermon are particularly compelling. Imagine that one encounters a fresh truth and sees the need to act. But this week is already booked and next week is busy, too. By the time there is a free space on the calendar, the call is forgotten and another chance is missed to get serious about serving God.

If we are serious about serving the Lord we must examine our calendar. Before the service opportunity arises we need to do the hard work of freeing up time in our schedules to commit to His work. This will allow us to take advantage of the opportunities that God places before us to serve. Don't misunderstand, there is a balance here. We cannot be at the mercy of the whims of the moment; neither can we be so rigid in our schedules that we can never respond to accept new service opportunities in our lives. Time must be prioritized. Think about the amount of time wasted watching TV.

Maybe singing in the choir is not as important as leading a Bible study or helping out with childcare. Pray about these things and make a list and prioritize your activities.

This rescheduling lays a foundation for a real life of service. Having secured the time away from your busy-ness you are able to find a place to serve. Often such opportunities will just fall into your lap as you go through life. You will encounter situations in which you can help. At other times you will need to seek out the needs of the church. Perhaps you are ready to volunteer to serve in the church and commit part of your life to helping others follow this walk with Christ. You can trust that as you are responsible with your time and as you use your life for God's purposes, God will open your eyes. God will give you the ability to see the needs around you as Jesus did, and from that will come the compassion to serve.

Financial planners commonly suggest that one should have enough money saved to pay six months' worth of bills. For many this seems an impossible dream. The principle however is simple enough. You can expect that something unexpected will happen. It always does. But only if you are prepared can you respond. The same is true with service. Jesus had a plan. He had a mission. Part of His mission included time for Himself and time with His disciples. But He structured His schedule so that when the ministry needs of the people came up He was ready to serve. This is not an easy task in our culture. Our culture teaches us that doing more and scheduling more gets us more. Jesus models the opposite. It is precisely because Jesus scheduled time for these activities that He was able to rest and pray and talk and laugh and care for other people.

Questions:

1. Have you ever found yourself too busy to help when asked?

2. What kinds of activities have taken up your time?

3. Which activities are unessential?

4. Try to anticipate what your schedule will look like after you are released from incarceration and make plans how you can serve others.

Day 7- A Reasonable Service
Read: Romans 12:1-8

As I write this devotional it is only a few days before Christmas. I want to get something for my wife but she insists that she doesn't need anything. What clothes she wants she will have a hard time finding, so fat chance that I can find anything for her. But what would you be able to give to God to show your gratitude for what He has done for you? What are you supposed to do for the One who created you then suffered and died to redeem you from eternity in hell? He doesn't need money. Nothing that you own is adequate to repay Him for what He has done. The answer is in this first verse in Romans 12. We are told to, *"Present your bodies a living sacrifice."* This is an acceptable service! How can that be? Does that mean we are supposed to die?

Clearly, all that we have, all that we are belongs to Christ. The only thing we have that He values is ourselves. Yes, we are supposed to die to self in our worldly pursuits so that we can offer ourselves to service in His kingdom without holding back. But God is generous, full of love and grace. He doesn't expect us to spend every hour of the day in prayer and worship. He knows that we must eat, clothe ourselves, house ourselves and care for each other. He expects us to marry and have children. He knows that we have to provide for the needs of our families and protect them. In fact, this is all part of His plan and our service to Him. We are to have a life that is balanced between the cares of this life and His eternal kingdom.

As a young man I had a difficult time realizing this. I thought I had to be doing church work, out winning souls and changing the world. While that is an important part of our service, the first and most important service is to provide for our families, meet our obligations to each other and live in harmony with our neighbors. If we don't get this right, if we neglect our families, then our outreach to the world is of little value and probably will not succeed.

The second part of this Scripture reference tells us how to make this possible. We are to change, to turn away from our old life and put on the new. By submitting ourselves to Christ we allow Him to transform our minds. By spending time with Him in prayer and study of His Word, by keeping our hearts and minds focused on Him and His kingdom He will change our way of thinking. He will give us a new set of values. It is like the metamorphosis that takes place between the caterpillar and the butterfly. The fuzzy worm actually dies to the old life and is transformed into a new creature. God calls us to be *"new creatures in Christ."* In Romans 6:1-14 Paul describes this as *"the old man being crucified with Him."* We are then raised from the dead so we can walk in newness of life. No longer do we present our bodies

"As instruments of unrighteousness to sin, but present yourselves to God as being alive from the dead, and your members as instruments of righteousness to God. For sin shall no longer have dominion over you."

This is your reasonable service.

Questions:

1. Have you been seeking after God only to have your own needs met?

2. What do you think God wants from you?

3. What parts of the "old Man" do you have to give up to be the new creature God wants you to be?

4. What things are holding you back from doing this?

STUDY 9 - INVENTORY

Day 1 – Discovering our Hidden Defects
Read: James 1:22-24; 1 Corinthians 11:28,31; 1 John 1:8

Let God search your heart. What sort of person are you? Can you be trusted? Are you kind and helpful to others. What does God expect of you? Are you selfish and self centered? Learning these truths is part of taking inventory. Most of us have heard about the Catholic confession where a person goes to a priest to tell him the sins they have committed. This is an important act for many Catholics, although fewer are practicing this regularly. Most of us want to hide our sins. We don't want to reveal them to a priest and certainly not to other people. Why are we called to confess? How does confession help us in our relationship with Jesus?

If God knows everything then He must also know about our sins, so why should we confess them? True, God knows our sins but often we do not. Confession is a time of self-examination. It helps make us aware of our shortcomings and failures. When we confess we are admitting that we are wrong and God is right. It makes us dependent on God in seeking to correct our behavior. Fortunately, God doesn't lay all our failures on us at one time. He knows we can't handle the sudden load. Thankfully, He gradually reveals them to us and expects us to work on continuous improvement. As we draw nearer to Him He makes us more aware of our remaining sins. It can become discouraging at times because it seems like the closer we get to Him the worse we seem to be.

It isn't that God is some kind of bully that insists on His own way, but by His very nature God cannot fellowship with the works of evil. Sin separates us from being in fellowship with Him. Therefore it is necessary to examine ourselves. Our personal growth and effectiveness are stifled as long as there is a rift in our fellowship with God. This rift is healed when we personally confess to God the offense that caused it. However, we have to understand that the regular confession of sins is not the basis of salvation once we become a Christ follower, it is the restoration of fellowship. It is our admission of error, but more importantly, that God is right. Our own way is prone to failure, but His way leads to life and righteousness.

God requires confession of sin as the means of maintaining a close personal walk with Him. He requires a continual acknowledgement of His Kingship; and confession of sin is the means by which you express your surrender to the sovereign will of God on a moment-by-moment basis. The regular confession of sin produces humility, a means of cleansing and renewing of the mind as well as deeper fellowship with God.

Often we are not aware of our sins or are unsure if what we are doing is displeasing to God. In your desire to be closer to Him you may need to pray that He will make you aware of anything in your life that needs to be confessed.

Questions:

1. Think about the sins that you need to confess. Maybe you want to write them down in a place where they won't be seen.

2. Are you ready to confess your sins to God and ask for His help in turning away from them?

Day 2 – Finding God in Our Everyday Life
Read: Jeremiah 29:14; Matthew 7:7-11

Seek and you will find. When we were children we played hide-and-go-seek. The best times were in the haymows of barns on the farms of family and friends. We all remember counting while everyone scattered to find good hiding places close to the base so we could slip in without being caught. Can you imagine playing the game if the seeker just sat on the base and never went looking? There wouldn't be any sense in playing the game, no excitement and no challenge. Living a life without adventure and challenge would be like playing such a game.

A large number of professing Christians are practical atheists.

They go about their day without realizing that God is part of their lives. They see the events of their lives as being the result of chance or coincidence. They fail to see that God is in control, that He is involved in their daily tasks, even when things don't go the way they think they should. They want to blame God for the bad things in life rather than seek to know how He is working on us through these difficult times. What can be an exciting adventure is left to a dull and mundane existence.

God wants to be involved in our lives. He wants to fellowship with us but we are not aware of His part in our lives. We need to be looking, seeking, asking, and knocking. Hebrews 13:2 tells us,

"Be not forgetful to entertain strangers: for thereby some have entertained angels unawares."

This is an exciting challenge! He also says that when we give a cup of cold water to a stranger it is the same as having given it to Him. Wow! What an opportunity we have to serve others, please God and store up heavenly rewards. We need to be attentive to the circumstances we face every minute of every day, looking for our God and Father in the everyday world. He shows Himself to us in many ways but we often excuse His intervention as coincidence. Even when we receive obvious answers to prayer, we rule out His supernatural intervention, thinking it would have worked out that way.

To find God in your everyday life, look back over the day's activities and events with the expectation that God is there. Give Him the credit when you get special help to do His work in the world. Look for the way He works through unusual timing, the things we often attribute to coincidence. The older and more experienced I get in living as a child of God, the less I believe in coincidence. Even when things do not go well, look for the lessons He is trying to teach you. Maybe He is allowing you to be tested to see if you are growing or to help you grow in a specific area of life. Ask Him for discernment and understanding as you seek to find and follow Him through your daily life. He is there and He wants you to live the exciting supernatural life of one of His children. If you have begun journaling, write these events down so you will be able to go back at a later time and see the many ways God has been working in your life.

Questions:

1. What recent event can you recall when you ask God for something only to attribute it to coincidence when it happened?

2. Think back over the last week and see if you can recognize God being involved in you life.

3. Have you begun journaling? If not, now would be a good time to start.

Day 3 – Common Misbeliefs
Read: Romans 1:18-32

With the virtually unlimited information available on the internet that can be published by anybody with a computer there is both a wealth of information and misinformation available. It often takes some careful searching to find the truth. For years I heard that the head of the patent office, Charles Duell, wrote to president McKinley in 1899 and suggested the patent office should be closed because everything that could be invented had been invented. Even President Reagan used this legend in one of his speeches. As it turns out, the story is untrue and probably the result of something said that was taken out of context.

Since so many e-mails are circulated making many absurd claims, a whole website called snopes.com has been dedicated to debunking them. One of the most recent false claims was that Senator O'Bama refused to pledge allegiance to the US flag. There is also a theory supposedly originating with Adolph Hitler called the *Big Lie*, "If you tell a lie, make it, big and tell it often people will believe it." While the source of this theory is questionable the end result is largely true. How many times have you believed something to be true only to find at a later time it was really false?

In our secular society where the supernatural power of God is denied, we live with many lies and half-truths, many of which we choose to believe because they suit or purposes. One of the greatest lies of all time is often heard by teenagers, "It is my life so let me live it my way and make my own mistakes, I don't need anybody else." Perhaps you have used this or even believe it. Who gave you life and cared for you when sick, fed you when hungry, bought you clothes, gave you a house in which to live, sent you to school and taught you how to talk, walk and drive? Do you not owe them something? What if there were no hospitals to set broken bones, no grocery store owners to sell you food, no police department or system of courts to protect you from more powerful people? If you think about it you will come to realize how totally false this notion really is. One look at the dysfunctional warlord's of the third world and we should fall to our knees and thank God that His Word stands in stark contrast to such antisocial evils that come about by the ways of man.

God made us social creatures and gave us governments to protect us, including marriage of one man and one woman for procreation and protection of children. Our culture has tried to destroy the institution of marriage in a number of ways. We have been taught that a woman who stays home to care for children is a second-class person, that love is something that happens to us beyond our control, that teenagers are going to have sex and drink alcohol so we should make sure they have contraceptives and told not to drink and drive. Secular society tells us that abortion is a right of women to control their own bodies. All of these lies and half-truths are told so that sex will be unrestricted and to minimize the consequences of immoral behavior. Our Scripture verse verifies this motive but also consider the words of Julian Huxley, once a leader of Darwinists, who said, "The reason we accepted Darwinism even without proof, is because we didn't want God to interfere with our sexual mores."

To make these lies believable we are told that the Bible is incorrect and full of myths, there is no God who created us, and all life is simply the result of time and chance. We are not responsible for our actions and can't help acting out because that is the way we were born or may be the result of a bad environment. My bad feelings justify bad actions, and medication can correct every ill. Many people walk around like zombies drugged up on Ridlin and anti-depressants with no hope of permanent recovery. Sin has become a politically incorrect word.

I frequently see a bumper sticker that says, "Question Authority." The intention is to rebel against the established authority of church and state, but this can be turned around to question those who display the sticker. It is time to question them about the new social order and ask what was really wrong with church and state. It worked well for over 200 years.

Now is the time to get to know God's Word and His plan for life on earth. Our life on earth is the testing ground to see if we are ready for heaven. Don't let yourself be fooled by the lies and half-truths like Satan used to beguile Eve. Now, turn to 1 Corinthians 2 where it says we have heavenly wisdom. It ends with an astounding declaration, "…we have the mind of Christ."

Questions:

1. Make a list of the lies that you read about here and thought were true.

2. How do you know whom to trust with the truth?

3. Why can't you always trust yourself?

4. How has this devotion changed your thinking about the American social order?

5. How does it make you feel knowing that the Holy Spirit gives you "the mind of Christ?"

Day 4 - Judging Others
Read: Matthew 7:1-5; Romans 14:1-21

I would never do a thing like that! She is such a wonderful person. Hitler should burn in hell. Our president is a liar. Correctional officers are all evil. How many times have you heard such statements made about other people, or made them yourself? This is called judging others. Yet, when others pass judgment on us we are quick to remind them of what Jesus said, "Judge not that you be not judged." Is that really what He meant? Does that mean we can't even pass judgment on the good things people do?

As we look at this passage and others like it, we have to understand both the subject of judgment and the intent of the statements. In Romans 14 Paul is speaking about judging others "over doubtful things." These are not matters of good or evil but about food sacrificed to idols and observance of holy days. In a later study we will consider the phrase, "In essentials unity, in nonessentials liberty, but in all things love." The practices described in Romans 14 are the nonessentials, what Paul calls doubtful things. This is clearly expressed in Romans 14:4-7 where we are warned not to judge another's servant over such things. In the thirteenth verse we are told, *"Therefore let us not judge one another anymore, but rather resolve this, not to put a stumbling block or a cause to fall in our brother's way."* This means we should not insist that others observe our practices or insist on our right to do things in their presence that would be offensive to them. This isn't hypocrisy as some might suppose, it is the showing of love and respect to those whose conscience might be offended. This is especially important when it comes to consumption of alcohol. This might not just offend other believers but it is especially troubling for those who have struggled with alcohol addiction.

Matthew 16 actually tells us to make judgments but also warns us to be careful how the judgments are made. This isn't a command not to judge, but a warning about how we make that judgement. We are warned to be careful in judging others because we will be judged with the same measure we use to judge others. We should start by taking inventory of our own weaknesses and failures so we are not blinded by them when judging others. It is much easier to find fault with other people while ignoring our own faults. The words of Leviticus 19:15 are beautiful. It says,

> *"You shall do no injustice in judgment. You shall not be partial to the poor, but in righteousness you shall judge your neighbor."*

As we take inventory we should ask the Holy Spirit to reveal our own faults and help us to overcome them.

Since we live in a world of good and evil we are expected to judge between truth and error. We need to recognize those who may lead us down the wrong paths. Without making judgment how can we *"beware of false prophets"* as we are told to do elsewhere in the

Bible? We must be able to determine for whom we should vote and whom to support or oppose based on our best understanding of their actions. We are even called to go to war against those who oppose righteousness or suffer the consequences should we judge the war to be unjust. Consider Leviticus 19:17,

> *"You shall not hate your brother in your heart. You shall surely rebuke your neighbor, and not bear sin because of him."*

When making judgments we must consider Matthew 7:20, *"By their fruits you will know them."* The fruit of the Spirit is given in Galatians 5:22-23.

Questions:

1. What does it mean to "not honor the person of the mighty?"

2. In what ways have you falsely judged other people?

3. In what ways have you failed to make judgments when you should have?

4. What specks are in your own eye that need to be removed?

5. How do you think other people will judge you if you "give them the finger?"

6. How does that make you feel?

Day 5 - Blowing Off Steam
Read: James 1:19-21; Galatians 5:18-25

During the eighteenth century the high-pressure steam engines were developed, primarily to pump water. It required great care to be sure the boiler did not become overheated. The excessive steam pressure would often cause the boiler to explode destroying the operator and everything nearby. Eventually a pressure valve was invented that allowed the excessive pressure to be safely released into the air. Thus, the term "blowing off steam" came to be applied to boilers as well as human reactions. Some modern psychologists equate our human behavior to the steam boiler advising that we must "blow off steam" rather than containing our frustrations until we have an uncontrollable outburst. That sounds reasonable, but it is often misinterpreted to mean that it is OK to blow-up and mis-behave when we are frustrated and angry. How does God expect us to handle disappointments, frustrations and outright anger?

What happens when we get angry and blow-up? Inevitably we hurt those around us. Nobody wants to be around those who are out-of-control. Blow-ups are marked by cursing, throwing things, and striking out at people around us, even those who had no part in the frustration. When I was a young man I was so foolish as to "punish" inanimate objects of my frustration, like my bicycle. Usually such frustrations are the result of our own shortcomings to which we do not want to admit. It is more convenient to blame the bicycle for breaking down than to blame myself for abusing it or failing to maintain it. I remember clearly when I was not more than fourteen years old, the pastor of the church next door dropped a tool he was using. His response was, "Bingo." I couldn't believe that this interruption did not bring a more dramatic response. How could he remain so calm when perplexed? I didn't realize this incident didn't bother him as it would have bothered me! He only needed to retrieve the tool and continue what he was doing.

God knows that His created beings are not machines incapable of self-control. Look at Galatians 5:23. We are told that the exercise of self-control is a fruit of the Spirit-filled life. The opposite is in verse 20, outbursts of wrath. He has given us the intelligence to manage our frustrations and He has given us His Holy Spirit to empower and comfort us. It is when we fail to appropriate these gifts from Him that we lose control and blow-up. Such reactions are the result of our being self-centered and intolerant. It is when we function as servants, giving ourselves to others, considering others more important than ourselves, that we find it possible to lower the temperature and pressure of our internal boilers so that blow-off and blow-ups are unnecessary. It isn't that we are expected to ignore frustrations. Rather than explode at another person we need to communicate in an appropriate way. Rather than telling them what wrong they have done to us we should tell them how badly we feel when such a thing is said or done.

When our frustration is due to chance circumstance we need to understand that God is in control. This is very hard to do as long as we see ourselves living in a secular world, a place where we are subject solely to chance and where God is not in control. In reality, He allows adversity into our lives so we can be refined, so we can learn self-control and exercise patience. We should learn to expect frustrations as part of life. What makes anyone think they should be spared adversity when everyone is affected at some time or in some way?

There are several ways you can deal with your internal anger. One is to direct it into physical activity. You can work it off in the gym or by running. In this way you turn your anger into a stronger and healthier body. You can also look for positive means to express yourself. In 1980 Cari Lightner was killed by a drunken driver. Her mother Candice said, "I promised myself on the day of Cari's death that I would fight to make this needless homicide count for something positive in the years ahead." In her campaign against drunk driving she became the organizer and founding president of Mothers Against Drunk Driving (MADD). When we endure adversity, with the help of God, a supernatural event takes place. Perhaps we will handle it like the pastor of the church next door or we will turn it into positive action like Candice Lightner. In any event we must learn self-control and never blow-up in such a way as to hurt those around us.

Questions:

1. How does God expect you to handle disappointments, frustrations and outright anger?

2. What things happen when you blow-up?

3. What positive result has ever occurred in your life as the result of a blow-up?

4. What can you do to overcome or channel anger and avoid negative results?

Day 6 - How to Change
Read: Romans 8:5-11

I was raised from childhood to believe in Christianity. My mother took us to church and Sunday school. But that was just weekly religion. It had little to do with my everyday living, especially when I reached my teens. But when I was in my twenties I came to know the Lord in a more personal way and began the struggle of changing my life to conform to the leading of the Holy Spirit. One of the many things for me to overcome was my addiction to cigarettes. I realized this habit had more control over me than the Holy Spirit and it had to go. It was something I struggled to overcome and went through numerous failures, but each time I repented and surrendered again to the Lord. Eventually, I realized that if I ever lit another cigarette I had never quit. Although I have been freed from this habit for more than 30 years and find the smell tobacco smoke to be offensive, I realize this habit once controlled me. Therefore, I resolve never to smoke another cigarette for the rest of my life. As was said previously, there is no magic pill for growth, but there are ways to pursue change if the desire is sincere.

Change is a scary thing. Maybe it seems like change is all this study series talks about. In the first day of Study 3 we talked about decision making and how that is part of change. Then in the first day of Study 5 we talked about God "growing us" and how that leads to change. In this devotion I want to deal with some of the more practical aspects of how to cause change to take place. In Romans 7 Paul mentions the struggle between the law and his actions. In verse 24 he desperately asks,

"Who will deliver me from this body of death?" In the next verse he gives the answer, "Through Jesus Christ our Lord...I myself will serve the law of God..."

First, we must recognize which of our actions are not pleasing to the Lord. Reading His Word and knowing His law makes this possible. Keeping the rules, the requirements of the law, isn't what saves us, it tells us what behavior needs to be changed. The dilemma is that we don't seem to be able to break the old habits. We often know our behavior is contrary to God's instructions for living but don't know how to change. It seems like we have no control.

We need to admit our weakness and ask Him to help. This requires a relationship with Him and honest communication. Submit to Him in prayer asking for the power of the Holy Spirit. Commit yourself to God and trust the Holy Spirit to work within you toward change. It also helps to confide in a trusted friend with your struggle and the change you have committed to make so you can be held accountable. Then do not give up when you fail.

One of the most important things is to avoid the people or situations in which you are likely to be tempted. You can also practice what you will say or do when tempted. For example, someone invites you to a bar to meet some friends, but you know you have a drinking problem. The common choice is to go along while telling yourself you won't take a drink. You may even fool yourself into thinking this will be an opportunity to tell you friends about Jesus. This is a bad decision because the next one will be to say, "Sure, I can have just one." Of course, we all know one will lead to another. Just decide now to say, "No, I have decided not to go there." Change requires some tough decisions. Remember, If nothing changes, nothing changes. This means your mind must be changed before you can expect a change in your actions.

Questions:

1. List at least three things that need to be changed in your life. Discuss these with your mentor.

2. What people or situations do you need to avoid to make these changes?

3. Think about and rehearse what you can say to avoid one of these tempting activities.

4. Even though you can't smoke in jail, are you still addicted to cigarettes? How can you "kick the habit" while still incarcerated?

Day 7 – Faith vs. Works
Read: Ephesians 2:8-9; James 2:20

In the television show "Touched by an Angel" there was an episode about a man who didn't believe in God. Eventually he was convinced that God did exist and if he didn't change his ways he was going to hell. He started doing things for other people and journaling, not in the usual way, but keeping a record of all the good things he did to assure himself that he wouldn't go to hell. The angels then had to explain to him that his good works would not get him to heaven, but that he had to have a relationship with God. Then the good works would follow as a result of that relationship. He struggled with this before he was finally able to understand.

Many people struggle with this idea. They even take offense at "do gooders" because they think such people are only serving themselves, working their way to heaven. Trying to do good works to earn our way to heaven is man's idea and it is completely contrary to God's plan. If we could earn salvation then Jesus would have suffered and died in vain. Our salvation would be dependent on our own works and we could boast about what we accomplished. What an insult to God and Jesus who knows the penalty of sin is death for eternity. If works can save us then how much money would it take?

C.S. Lewis explains in *The Lion the Witch and the Wardrobe* "every traitor (law breaker) belongs to me (the devil) …. Unless I have blood as the Law says, all Narnia (creation) will be overturned and perish…." Lewis is illustrating through this allegory that Satan has claim to all who sin and they can only be redeemed by the shedding of innocent blood. Only Jesus was free of sin and able to give Himself to break this bondage we have to Satan. In the Old Testament the Israelites offered unblemished lambs as an act of obedience that symbolized the death of Jesus until He came and completed the salvation that God had planned since the beginning of time.

So, if we are saved by faith then why do works? Some people still believe that all they have to do is "believe in Jesus and confess Him" and they will be saved no matter what else happens. What they do not realize is that "believing" and "accepting" demands obedience. Jesus commands us to love our neighbors and to go unto all the world baptizing in the name of Jesus. So what happens if we don't? Does this mean we lose that salvation we received when we believed? No, it means we never really believed or that we don't understand what it means to believe. When we truly believe, we are surrendering our lives to Jesus and allowing Him to come in and teach us how to live. We become alive to Him and die to self and sin. We give up disobedience and the old life to live anew for Him. Then we become enlisted in the King's army and live to serve Him and others. So salvation comes by faith and works are the evidence of that faith.

"The wages of sin is death, but the gift of God is eternal life in Christ Jesus our Lord." Romans 6:23.

Questions:

1. If it was illegal to be a Christian what evidence in your life could be used to convict You?

2. Considering that salvation is a gift from God and not of works, how does this change your attitude toward works?

STUDY 10 - FUNDAMENTALS OF THE FAITH

Day 1 - Unity in the Faith
Read: Ephesians 4:4-6

Driving down the street you will pass dozens of churches, each with a different name and denomination. Some of the denominations will even be different, like the Lutheran Church of America and the Lutheran Church Missouri Synod. Maybe you will see American Baptist or Southern Baptist. Sometimes there is no denominational name, like the

Congregational Free Church. Why are there so many different churches? Is there one that is right in all their beliefs? Some people see this apparent division and take the position that no one can be completely right. It would appear that all these churches are at odds with one another or that the truth cannot be fully known. Isn't this a blight on Christianity? Which church should you belong to?

Most all of those churches accepting Jesus as God and Savior belong to the Christian faith. Each one has its own practices and observances. Some practice different forms of communion. The Catholic Church has communion in every mass, every day of the week. Others practice communion weekly. Others commune less frequently. The Catholic Church believes the bread and the wine actually become the body and blood of Jesus when it is blessed, while most believe it remains bread and juice and is only symbolic of the body and blood of Jesus.

When it comes to baptism there is also a wide range of practices. Some churches baptize by sprinkling and others by complete immersion in water. A large number refuse to baptize infants and toddlers because they believe baptism has to be decided in the heart and requires a degree of understanding that young children neither have nor need for salvation. There is even disagreement on whether salvation is by baptism or that baptism is a sign that salvation has already taken place. I am sorry to say that some church people will deny that one is baptized at all unless the right words are pronounced in the ceremony. If you think these differences are bad, consider how much worse it would be to have only one all powerful church that forced you to believe and follow their practices or they would kill you. Such non-Christian religious groups exist in the world today. In fact, they even kill those of their faith belonging to a different denomination.

On the other hand, a few churches have taken a path of non-belief for the sake of unity. They have given up the principles of the faith in order to unite under one name or under one roof. They have surrendered truth for the sake of unity. In reality, it isn't just those differences that divide us, it is where we put our focus. We can focus on the differences or on those beliefs we hold in common. For example, all Christian faiths believe in baptism, so we agree that baptism is good. We do not have to coerce someone else to baptize using our methodology. All true

Christian faiths believe in communion. It really doesn't matter whether the communicant believes the emblems become the actual body and blood of Jesus. What matters is that we respect the belief of others and not do anything that would offend them or cause them to doubt (I Corinthians 8:9).

All of this can be very confusing and discouraging to the new Christian who simply wants to follow Jesus and do the right thing. Fortunately, God is not as small as we try to make Him. The important thing is that we all baptize, that we all have communion, that we are all saved by the Grace of God. You can decide for yourself what individual non-essential practice makes you comfortable.

Many other theological positions divide us into different churches and practices, but true Christianity will, for the most part, agree on essential tenets of the faith among which are:

- God the creator exists and has revealed Himself as the Father, Son and Holy Spirit,
- Salvation is a free gift that cannot be earned by works,

- Jesus was victorious over death and lives in the hearts of believers,
- We confess Him and are obedient to be baptized with water,
- We receive communion to celebrate Jesus' death,
- Sex outside the marriage relationship is an offense to God,
- Marriage of a man to a woman is ordained by God.

Questions:

1. Have you wondered about which is the true church? Has this kept you from accepting any of them?

2. Do you need to be baptized? If so, when can you plan to make this happen? Talk to your mentor about this.

3. Have you thought that you had to earn salvation by good works? How did this make you feel?

4. Are you ready to follow Jesus' with regard to sexual purity?

Day 2 - Baptism
Read: Romans 6:3-4

"There was a man sent from God whose name was John. This man came for a witness, to bear witness of the light, that all men through him might believe." John 1:8

John was born six months before Jesus. He lived in the Judean wilderness clothed in camel's hair and wearing a leather belt around his waist. His food was locusts and wild honey. Despite his remote location, people came from the whole region to hear him. Soldiers came to him asking what they should do since they swore allegiance to Rome. The religious leaders came out to hear and question him. Even the tax collectors came to hear him. People came out to hear his message and to be baptized. He said,

"I indeed baptize with water, but One mightier than I is coming, whose sandal strap I am not worthy to loose. He will baptize you with the Holy Spirit and fire."

Nevertheless, John the Baptist was also to baptize Jesus, the Son of God. At this baptism, heaven was opened and the Holy Spirit descended in bodily form like a dove upon Him. A voice came from heaven that said,

"You are my beloved Son, in You I am well pleased."

All Christian churches practice baptism in one form or another. While some teach that baptism is essential for salvation, others believe it is simply a sign of obedience. Some pour water on the individual while others insist on complete immersion. Some baptize infants and others baptize only those who are old enough to confess Christ as Lord. Some Christians who were baptized as infants want to be baptized again as an understanding adult. It is not my intention to tell you exactly what you should believe, only to encourage you to study the Bible, pray about it and make a decision with which you are comfortable. God knows your heart and will honor your sincere desire to follow Jesus if it is derived from Scripture, prayer, and the Holy Spirit in you.

Baptism portrays what you believe about Jesus, what He has done for you, and that you want to live a new life as one of His followers. It is a demonstration of the faith you profess. It is a sign of obedience to the commands of Jesus. Baptism unites you to Him in an intimate way. In the reading for today the Bible tells us through baptism we are buried with Him into His death, that just as Christ was raised from the dead we also shall be raised to a new life. While faith must come first, it should lead right into baptism as the beginning of the believers walk with Christ. Baptism is not a work of salvation, (although some would disagree) it is a demonstration of our acceptance of Christ and our trust for Him to be in control of our lives. How could a believer not want to do this?

It is a common misconception that one is baptized into a particular church. I clearly remember my childhood friends saying, "I was baptized Catholic," or "I was baptized Methodist." In reality, we are baptized into Christ. It has little to do with the denomination except which format is used. While some people prefer to be baptized by a pastor or priest, any Christian can perform a baptism at any time and in any place. In the book of Acts, Philip baptized the Ethiopian eunuch on the side of the road. Paul baptized the Philippian jailer and his household after an earthquake broke open the jail where he was being held. Don't put it off until you think you have finally reached a certain spiritual level. There isn't a "right" time or place except the present. With the baptism you will receive the power of the Holy Spirit that will be an essential help in becoming the kind of person God wants you to be.

Questions:

1. Where you baptized as a baby, an adult, or not at all?

2. Are you comfortable with this arrangement?

3. What action do you need to take as a result of your answer?

Day 3 - Communion
Read: I Corinthians 11:23-26

During the time of Jacob, God knew that famine would be coming to the land of Canaan. Through a series of troublesome events He sent Jacob's son, Joseph to the land of Egypt. Again, through the mighty hand of God, Joseph became a powerful leader in Egypt and invited the rest of his family (75 in all) to live with him there in the region of Goshen. Over the next 300 years Jacob's family thrived and became a large nation. The Egyptians felt threatened by their numbers and prosperity so they arranged to bring them under slavery.

God raised up Moses to deliver them from oppression and return them to the land of Canaan (now known as Israel). God used a series of natural disasters to force Pharaoh to release the Israelites. The last was the most significant, where the angel of death claimed the firstborn of every family unless the blood of the sacrificial lamb was painted on the doorpost of the house. This event led to the celebration of Passover which has been observed by the Jews to this day. It is also the forerunner of the communion celebrated by Christians since the last supper of Christ. It continues to be celebrated by Christian believers until this day and will continue until the return of Christ. You may wonder how these observances are connected.

During the time of the Passover celebration Jesus was staying in the town of Bethany, just outside Jerusalem. He sent two of His disciples into Jerusalem to secure a room where He could observe the occasion with His twelve disciples. At the end of the dinner, the bread Jesus took was the matzah (unleavened bread) of the Passover. He then broke it and gave it to the disciples saying,

"Take and eat, this is my body given for you and for many."

Then he took the cup of wine and said,

"Take and drink, this is my blood shed for the remission of sins."

Afterward, He left for the Garden of Gethsemane where he prayed and was betrayed by Judas into the hands of the Jewish leaders. From there He was beaten and crucified on the cross. Although it wasn't understood at this time by His disciples, this sacrifice of His life was a fulfillment of the elements used in the Passover observance. The matzah Jesus offered was that piece that was hidden until the end of Passover, just as Christ was the hidden bread of heaven that was finally revealed at the Last Supper. The cup of wine was the third cup in the Seder (Passover meal) that was called the cup of redemption, just as Christ became the Redeemer. Jesus became the fulfillment of the Passover lamb. It was His blood that was given to save us all. God had determined all these things more than 1500 years before the coming of Jesus, even before the world began.

The report of the Last Supper is recorded in all four of the Gospels. Three of them relate the giving of the bread and the wine as His body and blood. However, the Gospel of John records Jesus as washing the disciples feet. A few Christian churches still practice foot washing as part of the communion service. Whether or not foot washing is practiced, the communion is received as a memorial of Christ's sacrifice. His blood delivers us from condemnation and death in the same way the Israelites were delivered from death during the Passover.

We are required to be holy. Jesus instituted communion as a memorial of His sacrifice that we should not forget it. He expects us to come solemnly. We are told to examine ourselves. We are about to receive emblems, representations of His body and His blood into our own bodies. We should prepare ourselves mentally and spiritually. In Mark 11:25 we are told to forgive others before we pray. We are told that God will not hear us if we harbor sin in our lives. Should we not therefore cleanse ourselves from any sin before receiving His body and blood? Communion is a celebration of our redemption from sin through the sacrifice of Jesus.

Questions:

1. Had you heard of the Passover meal before?

2. How does it make a difference to you to realize that Passover is symbolic of the coming of Jesus?

3. How do you feel about being able to celebrate Jesus' death by taking communion?

Day 4 - Knowing God's Will
Read: Judges 6:36-40; James 4:1-3

Have you ever wondered, "How can I know God's will?" What choices would God want me to make? Gideon asked the same thing in the text you just read. What he did is described today as "laying a fleece before God." Although God wants us to seek His will in prayer, there are times when we may choose as Gideon did to propose some circumstance and outcome by which we will know what God wants us to do. Unlike Gideon, we need to be sure we will take the outcome as being God's direction for us and abide by it.

I remember a time in 1970 when my wife and I felt led to leave our hometown, our nice new house, family and friends to take a job in another part of the country. We prayed earnestly that God would show us whether this was His will for our lives, but we had nobody interested in buying our house. Finally, I "laid the fleece." I proposed that if this was His will then we would get an offer to buy our house. I agreed that the offer would not have to be acceptable, just an offer. The next week we received our first offer, albeit unacceptable. We were encouraged then to know we were doing the right thing even after the new company where I had gone to work went bankrupt! God had a purpose in placing us where we were during that time of our lives and would later lead us to another part of the country.

Many times we have to discern the difference between our own desires, wants and inclinations with God's will. We not only have to determine what choices to make, but have the courage to carry them out, even when the circumstances are against us. Maybe the right decision is going to cost us money. Maybe it will require us to draw away from some unhealthy relationships with ungodly people. For example, His will regarding our relationships is clearly found in His Word. In James 4:1-4, there is a description of desires and behaviors that will destroy good relationships. The issue is whether we will allow the world's values and circumstances to control our choices. God will honor those decisions we make after sincerely seeking His direction through the Word, prayer and advice from other sincere believers.

Everyday we are faced with issues large and small. When do we find it necessary to seek God's will? Is it only with major issues or small ones as well? As we spend time with God in daily devotions it is a time to commit our lives to Him and ask for His help in facing issues of the day. This is why it is best to spend time with Him in the morning, before the day unfolds. As we grow in practicing our faith we should be able to function without asking about every little detail of life, what we should eat for breakfast, what clothes we should wear, whether we should go to work or not. If we are submitting daily to Him, He will be there in the small events. I remember one time on a business trip I decided not to wear a tie while visiting a company. I did not know why I made the decision but God's hand in it became evident when I overheard the business associate telling somebody, "I knew he could be trusted when he showed up without a tie."

However, when it comes to larger issues, like should I buy a new car, a used one, or none at all; this should be discussed with Him and not a snap decision. Ultimately, we need to be sure we are yielded to Him and ready to take the way He leads even when it isn't the most comfortable and convenient path we would chose.

Questions and Actions:

1. What major decision have you made without seeking God's will and how did it work for you?

2. Maybe you are facing some tough decisions about maintaining unhealthy relationships. Are you ready to follow Christ's leadership?

3. List some areas that need to be yielded to the will of God.

Further Reading: First John 2:15-17

Day 5 – Assurance of Salvation
Read: 1 John 5:11-13

As a teenager I used to contemplate that if I lived to be 80 I would have until I was 40 years to set my life straight with God. I would have the last half of my life to balance all the bad things I had done in the first half. Besides the fact that my concept of how to get to heaven was flawed, I was making a huge assumption that I would live to be eighty. Many people are offended when they hear a Christian say, "I know I am going to heaven when I die." They are offended because they do not understand the process by which we are saved. They think the person making the claim is being presumptuous, that the person thinks he is "good enough" to go to heaven. The problem in dealing with this issue is that most people are wrong in their understanding about salvation.

We really have only one way to know the truth and that is from the Bible. Unfortunately, the Bible speaks about it in different ways. As in the reading above from 1John, the Bible says you may know you have eternal life. However, in several other places the Bible talks about those who are "being saved." Whether you are sure about your salvation or not will not make a difference in whether you are saved in the end, but it will make a difference in what you believe about God and how you live. For that reason some would say this is one of the essential issues concerning our faith.

First, we need to make it clear that salvation is not something we are able to earn by our own works. If that were true then Christ would not have had to die on the cross. The Bible is very clear that God declares those who believe in Jesus' redemptive sacrifice to be righteous. In Ephesians 2:8-9 the Bible says that salvation is a gift from God and is not the result of any work that we can do. Once we see that salvation does not depend on us, the issue is much easier to understand.

Another thing that will help in understanding this topic is that the Bible speaks from two different perspectives. One is our position in Christ, we have been declared righteous. God knows the outcome. But from our perspective we are in the process of being saved. This explains what it means when it says we are "being saved," or in another place that we are to "work out our own salvation."

The word "saved" is in the past tense. It is something that already happened. Scripture says we have become children of God, that we are adopted into His family, not by what we profess to believe, but how we think and live. God doesn't disinherit us every time we sin and then adopt us again when we confess the sin. Our names are written in the Book of Life with permanent ink.

These are ideas of what has happened, not those things that are coming to pass. So you may ask, "Can salvation be taken away. Can we lose it?" No, God is sovereign. What He has done cannot be undone as long as we continue in the faith. This means our sins of the past, present and future are covered as long as we call upon the blood of Jesus. Our salvation is not the result of a religious experience but of a continuing relationship with God. The final question is, "Will God allow His children to deny Him?" The best way to answer this is never to deny Him and don't try to answer this question regarding somebody else's salvation.

Questions:

1. What would you say to the person who claims they have been saved and now will go to heaven no matter what terrible things they might do?

2. How does it make you feel to know that your salvation cannot be taken from you?

3. How can you deepen your relationship with God?

Day 6 – Trinity
Read: Romans 8:9-11

The teaching of the Trinity is one of the most problematic doctrines of Christianity. There are those who deny the triune nature of God. In fact, they are even insulted at the idea of three natures and strenuously oppose it. In their mind this is the same as polytheism (many gods). They claim that the word "trinity" does not occur in Scripture, and that is true. They also say it is a concept invented in the fourth century when it was formally described in a doctrinal statement. They say they believe in Jesus, but that Jesus is not a separate member of the Godhead. They believe that the Holy Spirit is simply God's power and Jesus is God's name, or only the Son of God without divinity. This error is understandable, as the concept of the Trinity cannot be fully grasped by our finite minds. However, as one carefully studies the Scripture in search of the truth, the doctrine of the Trinity becomes the only explanation of God's nature. The reading for today is one of many that can only be explained by the Trinity.

Trinity is a term we have created to describe the complex nature of God who reveals Himself in three distinctly different ways. God is spirit and is described as the Father. He revealed Himself and took on a human body when He came to earth as the Son, Jesus, and God lives in us, empowers us and guides us by His Spirit, described in the reading today as from God and as the Christ. Consider the reading for today along with John 14:26 that says,

"But when the Father sends the Advocate as my representative, that is the Holy Spirit, he will teach you everything and will remind you of everything I have told you," and in John 15:26, "But I will send you the Advocate, the Spirit of truth. He will come to you from the Father and will testify all about me."

It becomes very difficult to arrive at any other explanation but that God the Father, the Son of God, and the Holy Spirit are one and the same with independent yet completely harmonious functions. They are one and three, a tri-unity.

Many of the epistles begin with the blessing, "Grace to you and peace from God our Father *and* the Lord Jesus Christ." Why would the apostles use both "God the Father" and the "Lord Jesus Christ" if they were one and the same? Why did God say in the great commission to, "baptize in the name of the Father, and of the Son, and of the Holy Spirit" if all three were one and the same person? All this can be very confusing, especially to the new believer, but the idea needs to be dealt with so you will not be surprised or unprepared at some future time when the subject comes up. In I Peter 3:15 we are told to "be ready always to give an answer to every man that asks you a reason for the hope that is in you with meekness and fear."

This devotion in no way fully deals with this issue of the Trinity, but it should help you understand that there is divergent thoughts and strong opinions about the nature of God. You should be prepared by carefully studying all of Scripture, praying for the truth, and allowing God to speak truth to your heart.

Questions:

1. What questions do you still have about the Trinity? Write them down and discuss them with your mentor.

2. Has this devotion caused you to think more clearly or only added more confusion for you?

3. What other Scripture references can you find that helps understand this subject?

Day 7 – Miracles
Read: John 11:1-44

Thirty-seven miracles of Jesus are recorded in the four Gospels, but raising Lazarus from the dead is only recorded in the Gospel of John. The purpose for this miracle is revealed by several verses, beginning in verse four. Jesus reveals that the sickness of Lazarus is "not unto death, but for the glory of God, that the Son of God may be glorified through it." Then Jesus appears to deliberately delay going to heal Lazarus while he was sick, but confesses in verses fourteen and fifteen that Lazarus is dead and, "I am glad for your sakes that I was not there, that you may believe." Jesus wanted to do more than heal Lazarus, He wanted to use this mighty miracle of raising a man from the dead to show who He really was, to demonstrate His mighty power. In verse 41 Jesus prays out loud before many witnesses, and in verse 42 He confesses that this was done

"because of the people standing by…that they may believe that You sent Me." This is very consistent with the theme of the Gospel of John proclaiming the deity of Jesus.

In Acts 5:12 it says, "Through the hands of the apostles many signs and wonders were done among the people." We repeatedly see the expression, "signs and wonders" in Acts, as God was doing many miraculous deeds through the apostles to build up the "Christian" church. In 1 Corinthians, starting near the end of Chapter 13, Paul describes miracles, healings, prophecy and tongues as being among the gifts God gives to His people to support the Body of Christ. There arose a controversy over the use of tongues that continues until this day. Some people insist that tongues are given to all believers when they receive the Holy Spirit. Others believe that God no longer uses tongues or healings, that these gifts were not needed after the apostolic age when the church was in its infancy. This latter position runs into problems when the other gifts mentioned are teaching, helps, administrations, and the greatest of all, the gift of Love.

Undoubtedly, these latter gifts continue to this day and this leaves one trying to make distinctions between gifts and miraculous signs and wonders, distinctions that are not made in the Bible.

According to [1] Geisler and Turek, true miracles are those unmistakable supernatural acts of God that cannot be explained by natural laws, natural forces, or anything else in the physical universe. Raising Lazarus from the dead or healing a person with Leprosy are examples of true miracles and are performed in the context of the power of God in accordance with His devine purpose or plan. God does not perform miracles for His mere entertainment.

On the other hand, those events of unusual timing and consequence we often describe as miracles are really acts of providence. As stated by Geisler and Turek, these are beneficial happenings arranged by God that may be quite remarkable and stimulate our faith, however, they can be explained by natural laws. An example of providential acts of God might be the survival of a person unharmed in a horribly destructive car crash.

Most of the miracles we read about in the Bible happened during specific times and for specific purposes associated with God's devine plan. The reason we don't see miracles today like those recorded in Biblical times is because God is not now confirming any new revelation to us. This doesn't mean God does not perform miracles today, just that He may not have the compelling reasons to display His power as was done in former times. On the other hand, we believe that God is in control and we see His devine providence working in our lives on a daily basis.

You are strongly encouraged to read *I Don't Have Enough Faith to be an Atheist,* by Norman Geisler and Frank Turek. There you will find a wealth of knowledge concerning the origin and truth of the universe.

Questions and actions:

1. What kind of miracles have you witnessed in your life?

---

[1] *"I Don't Have Enough Faith to be an Atheist, "* by Norman Geisler and Frank Turek

2. Have you ever prayed for a miracle and then explained it away as coincidental? What kind of miracle might this have been?

Further Study: "*I Don't Have Enough Faith to be an Atheist,*" by Norman Geisler and Frank Turek

STUDY 11 - ARE WE THERE YET?

Day 1 – Looking Back
Read: James 1:2-8

I often take trips into the Canadian wilderness so I work out at the gym, walking and swimming in order to maintain a strong physical condition for my wilderness adventures. On a trip in 2007 I decided to test myself by swimming about 3/4 of a mile across Scotia Lake. I arranged to have a safety boat in case I ran into any difficulty. I kept my eye on a rock at the far shore as I stroked along, sometimes doing the breaststroke and then rotating over to a more relaxing backstroke. As I watched the rock it just didn't seem to be getting any closer. On I went, but the progress seemed painfully slow. With impatience I eventually looked back at my starting point and was greatly encouraged. I could see I had come much further than I perceived by looking ahead at my goal. Well, to finish the story, I made it to the other shore before turning around and swimming part way back again. Again, the impatience won me over and I took a boat ride back to camp.

Our spiritual journey is much like my swimming test. Spiritual growth is slow. The process takes time. We become impatient wanting to see instant progress. Looking forward to the goal it doesn't look like we are getting any closer. This is what growing in Christ is like. Thankfully, God does not expect us to be perfect instantly, just like we don't go from childhood to adulthood in a single day. He knows it requires growth over time. Fortunately, He is more patient than we are. He will only challenge us with what we can handle at the moment, day by day. As we overcome sin and mature in our walk He reveals new areas that need to be brought under submission. Being constantly aware of new shortcomings in our lives can cause us to become discouraged. Looking back to where we started and seeing the change that has taken place helps us realize that God really is at work in our lives.

Whether you are recovering from a life of substance abuse, mending broken relationships, rebuilding your life of brokenness, planning a career and seeking to become more like Jesus, it is important to keep your eye on the goal. At the same time it is useful to look back to see the progress you have made. Remember what it was like before coming to Christ. We live in a society of instant gratification, "I want what I want when I want it." But God has called us to live a life of patience, longsuffering, consistency and purpose. The book of James also says in verse 12, *"God blesses those who patiently endure testing and temptation. Afterward they will receive the crown of life that God has promised to those who love Him."* Do not be afraid to turn to Him and ask for His help. We can only find victory as we depend upon Him for our strength.

Questions and Activities:

1. Since becoming a believer have you set goals that you want to achieve?

2. Take a minute to list at least three goals you want to set for yourself.

3. Do any of these goals seem impossible to achieve?

4. Set reasonable dates for achieving each goal and go over them with your mentor.

5. Have you ever become discouraged at achieving a goal and given up before asking for help?

Day 2 – God is Faithful

Read: 1 Kings 8:23-24 & 56; Hebrews 13:5; Joshua 1:5 & 9

There is a poem that was written in 1936 by Mary Stevenson that expresses God's faithfulness.

One night I dreamed I was walking along the beach with the Lord. Many scenes from my life flashed across the sky. In each scene I noticed footprints in the sand. Sometimes there were two sets of footprints, other times there was one only. This bothered me because I noticed that during the low periods of my life, when I was suffering from anguish, sorrow or defeat, I could see only one set of footprints, so I said to the Lord, "You promised me Lord, that if I followed you, you would walk with me always. But I have noticed that during the most trying periods of my life there has only been one set of footprints in the sand. Why, when I needed you most, have you not been there for me?" The Lord replied, "The years when you have seen only one set of footprints, my child, is when I carried you."

Our life is a journey. At times it is exciting and other times it becomes boring, even frightening as those difficult periods mentioned in the poem by Mary Stevenson. If you continue to look up to God and trust Him for the strength to carry on, even the drudgery can become exciting. You can learn to live each day in expectation of what God can and will do. To do this you need to understand God's faithfulness, that He will not abandon you or expect you to do more than you are able. God being faithful does not mean you will never suffer hardship, or that you will not be disappointed. It means He is consistent, that He will keep His promises. His faithfulness is best seen when you observe Him throughout the history of mankind. To do this you need to read the whole Bible where you will discover a picture of His faithfulness and the promises He has kept (See Appendix III for a read through schedule).

Faithfulness is an essential part of God's divine character. God is true. He cannot lie. His Word of promise is a sure thing. No one yet ever trusted Him in vain. We find this precious truth expressed almost everywhere in the Scriptures, for His people need to know that. But it is one thing to accept the faithfulness of God as a Divine truth, it is quite another *to act upon it*. God has given us many "exceedingly great and precious promises," but how many times do we doubt His fulfillment of them? Are we really *expecting* Him to do for us all that He has said and what we have seen Him do for others?

God's faithfulness and promises are at times dependent on our acceptance of them. While God forgives us out of grace and unconditional love, His promises are usually given with conditions. He is not going to give us everything He promised if we do not remain faithful to Him. This is seen frequently with the promises He makes to Israel as you read in the text for today.

Questions and Activities:

1. Make a list of God's promises that you rely upon.

2. To receive His promises, what does God expect from you?

3. If you have read the entire Bible, commit to reading it again or begin reading it for the first time. There is a Bible read through schedule in Appendix III.

4. Do you think God will be less faithful to you than to those we read about in the Bible?

Further study: *Autobiography of George Mueller*

Day 3 – I Never Promised You a Rose Garden
Read: 2 Corinthians 12:7-10

Turn on the radio or television and you are certain to hear the Gospel of prosperity. "Turn your life over to Jesus and He will take care of everything," they say. He will heal you and there will be no more pain and suffering. I have heard some say that God will heal us from every infirmity if we just have enough faith. As much as these people firmly believe what they are saying, both the facts of life and the Bible say otherwise. True, God does heal us, and will continue to heal us except for that final illness that results in physical death. So far, death is 100% certain. The record shows that nobody lives on planet earth forever.

Of all the people that we would expect God to heal it would be the apostle Paul. He was a missionary extraordinaire and wrote a large part of the New Testament. But Paul didn't live in a rose garden either. As was described in the reading for today, he suffered an infirmity from which he was not healed even though he pleaded with God three times. We don't know for sure, but evidence from other verses hint that his eyesight was probably permanently affected when he was blinded on the road to Damascus. Clearly, God didn't heal him because He wanted to use that infirmity to humble Paul and remind him of his dependence on God. If we go back a little further in 2 Corinthians 11:24-28, we see that Paul also suffered greatly for his witness of Jesus. Should we expect anything better?

It is easy to fall for this prosperity gospel. Didn't Jesus say,

"My yoke is easy and my burden is light?"

Didn't He say,

"I have come that you will have life and have it more abundantly."

If Jesus wasn't preaching the gospel of prosperity then what did He mean? You were warned at the beginning of this study series not to take Scripture out of context. In the Bible Jesus also says, "I came not to bring peace but the sword" (Matthew 10:34). Early believers were persecuted and murdered for their faith. The persecution continues around the world even in this presumably enlightened era. As I write, Christians in Orissa, India are being hunted down and killed simply because they are teaching a doctrine that isn't Hindu. Following Christ does not guarantee us a life of peace and ease, but His faithfulness assures us that He will be with us through all circumstances.

Questions and activities:

1. Have you turned to Jesus to deliver you from your troubles or to help you through them?

2. How do you feel knowing that following Jesus may not be so easy?

3. Is your faith worth dying for?

4. List three things that you expect Jesus to help you through. Discuss these with your mentor.

Day 4 – When Will Jesus Come Again?
Read: Matthew 25:1-13

[2]Heaven's Gate was the name of an American religious group led by Marshall Applewhite and Bonnie Nettles. They believed that the planet Earth was about to be recycled (wiped clean, refurbished and rejuvenated), and that the only chance to survive was to leave it immediately. The group's end coincided with the appearance of comet Hale-Bopp in 1997. Applewhite convinced thirty-eight followers to commit suicide so that their souls could take a ride on a spaceship that they believed was hiding behind the comet, carrying Jesus.

How many times have we heard about groups who thought they knew the time of Jesus Christ's return and they gathered at a special place to receive Him. In the first century some of the converts to Christ thought His return was eminent. They didn't work or do anything but sit around consuming what resources they had while waiting for His return. All of those who followed false prophets fell into this error ending with loss, even of life. How are we to avoid repeating such errors as these?

First, by understanding that we will not know the day and the hour of His return. Acts 1:7 says,

"It is not for you to know the times and seasons which the Father has put under His own authority."

Anyone that proposes to know is a liar. Jesus told His disciples that no one knows the day and hour but the Father (Matthew 24:36). He also said that we can recognize the signs of His coming so we will not be surprised. The Bible makes it clear that Jesus will return so we should always be ready.

It is clear that God doesn't want us to know the exact hour. One reason is that by knowing we would put off our commitment to Him until the time was upon us. He wants us to continue living for Him,

---

[2] Source Wikipedia

taking the Gospel message to others with the same urgency as though He was coming today. However, He delays coming to allow time for more to receive salvation. He wants everyone to have a chance of coming to Him before it is too late.

Secondly, by knowing that we do not need to go and find Him, He will find us. It is clear in Matthew 24:30-31 that we do not need to be in any special place. Wherever we are He will find us. It is rather foolish to think we have to find Him. As He ascended, He made it clear that there will not be any special place for us to meet Him when He comes for us in the clouds.

Finally, by being ready at all times as it says in Matthew 24:45. We will never be surprised if we are expecting Him at any moment, and that means living and serving as though He was already here. That is His expectation for the way we should be living.

Questions:

1. What reasons do you want Jesus to return today?

2. What reasons would you want Him to delay His return?

3. What did you think when you heard of some group that went to a place for Jesus' return only to be disappointed?

4. Why do you suppose Jesus delays coming?

5. What will you do to be ready for His return?

Day 5 – Victory in Christ
Read: 1 Corinthians 15:54-58

One of the frustrations of jail ministry is developing a relationship with a person who comes to Christ during incarceration only to see them leave jail and return to their former life as though nothing happened to transform them. I have seen people able to pray great prayers and quote Scripture, completely abandon all the good plans they made while incarcerated. For this reason transitional houses have been opened in some venues where those leaving jail can live until they establish a Christian lifestyle outside the institution. Even in the transitional houses we have seen them quickly compromise their faith and abandon the commitments they made to complete the program. Sometimes this is because they have a small disagreement with somebody in the house. At other times they choose to leave when tempted with independence or worldly pursuits. In all cases it is because they have not completely surrendered their lives to the Lordship of Jesus and remained true to the commitments they have made. How can you avoid being one of these casualties?

In your former life you lived by compulsive behavior, but now you are called to a new life of submission and obedience. This means letting Christ control every area of your life. Yielding to Christ living in you will give victory over sin and Satan. Satan will try to ruin you by putting wrong thoughts in your mind, but Scripture is the weapon against Satan's lies. That is why the apostle Paul says in 2 Corinthians 12:10, *"For when I am weak, then I am strong."* God's strength is made perfect on our weakness. When we rely on self instead of God and His Word we are going to fail.

Perhaps those of us in ministry expect too much from our protégées. It is difficult to come out of the world and immediately begin to understand and live the Christian lifestyle. Even long-time Christians have their failures. But that is the purpose of this study series and the mentoring program, to help you reach a maturity level consistent with the purposes of God before you are enticed away by the enemy. This is the victory! In the past we let our dependence on people and things determine our self-worth and identity. Victory is obtained by transferring our dependency from self to claim the victory that is ours in Christ. In Philippians 4:13 it says, *"I can do all things through Christ who strengthens me."* When we neglect His Word and rely on self we are prone to failure. We must live to please God instead of self and other people. It is all about Him.

In the reading for today the final victory over death is described. This is when we remain faithful to the very end of life. This is the time that eternal life is transformed from a promise to reality. Death will not conquer the faithful but we shall receive immortality where there is no fear, no more temptations, no anxiety, no more loneliness or tears, no more hatred or violence. What a glorious time that will be and what a contrast between heaven and hell!

Questions:

1. What are some of the lies Satan uses to defeat you?

2. What compulsive behaviors controlled your former life?

3. How can you be weak and strong at the same time?

4. What promises have you made and broken?

5. How has that worked for you?

Day 6 - The Truth About Hell
Read: Matthew 25:31-46; Revelation 20:7-13

Many people have great difficulty with the concept of hell. They ask, "How can a loving God punish a person forever?" I have even heard it said that hell is not consistent with God's character of love and grace. They especially have trouble when dealing with loved ones or "good" friends that die without Christ. However, the Bible makes it clear that hell is a reality and that certain people will go there along with the beast and the false prophet mentioned in the verse above.

Some of the problem about judging is we cannot trust our own judgment. We already talked about the problem of judging others. We have to trust that God is wiser than we are and He will not unjustly allow undeserving people to spend eternity in hell. We also have to understand that God will not force Himself on people. He has graciously provided a way and that provision cost Him dearly through the suffering and death of His precious Son, Jesus. People who reject that provision and choose to live apart from God do so to satisfy their own evil nature and desires. They don't want a relationship with Him, to pray, go to church or participate in Bible studies. They find these practices dull and useless. If they do not enjoy God in this life why would they want to spend eternity with Him in heaven? You see, it is not God who condemns people to hell, they make a choice to go there on their own.

But what about people who don't believe there is a God but live good lives helping other people? Is it fair that such people should go to hell? This thinking is the result of two errors. One is that we are again putting ourselves in the judgment seat, saying who is good and who is not. Only God knows the heart and can make that determination. The other error is that we seem to think that heaven is the reservation for good people and hell is punishment for the bad. If it were that simple then Jesus would not have come to earth to suffer and die to redeem us. We could do it ourselves. In reality, when sin came into the creation man was destined to eternal death. That is what God explained to Adam and Eve. Although not clearly understood by all believers, this is what is meant by the term "original sin."

This truth is very well expressed in *The Lion, the Witch and the Wardrobe*, by C.S. Lewis. The witch (Satan) tells the lion (Jesus) that he knows the law that was written when the world began that makes every traitor (sinner) her lawful prey, that for every treachery (sin) she has the right to a kill. But it goes on to explain in a subsequent chapter a deeper secret of the law from before the world began, that if a willing victim was killed in place of the traitor, "Death would itself start working backward." The innocent blood would redeem the sinner from the law of eternal death. God used the blood of innocent animals to cover the sins of the believers until the time of Jesus was fulfilled and His perfect life was given by sacrifice on the cross. His blood did more than temporarily cover sins, it completely removed them. This opened heaven's door for all believers to enter from Adam to the end of time.

We find two judgments mentioned in the Bible. The Great White Throne judgment was mentioned in the reading from Revelation. This judgment is reserved for all those who rejected Jesus the Christ, God's precious sacrifice offered for the redemption of the world. Those who rejected the precious blood of Jesus, who heard the truth and were unwilling to simply believe, will be cast into eternal damnation. The other judgment is for the believers (1 Corintians 3:13-15). In this judgment those whose names are recorded in the Book of Life will be saved. However, their works will be tried by fire and only those things worthy will remain.

Questions:

1. How does it make you feel to know that as a believer you will not be condemned to hell?

2. Once your name is written into the "Book of Life" why can't you go on living the way you did in the past?

3. Does this devotion answer your questions about hell? Discuss any questions with your mentor.

Day 7 – Becoming What We Are
Read: 1 John 3:1-3

When a child is born to citizens of the United States or born to noncitizens on US soil, that child becomes a citizen of the United States even though the opportunity to exercise that citizenship has never been acted upon. In the same way, loyalty to our country or anything else cannot be measured at less than 100%. You are either loyal or you are a traitor. There is no way to be 50% loyal. When you are born again you receive a similar status in the Kingdom of Heaven. Our Scripture reading today assures that you have received eternal life. This is your position in the Kingdom of God. This being true, then we ask, "What is the purpose of obedience?" Why am I expected to grow in Christ?" What does the Scripture in Philippians 1:6 mean where it says:

> *"I am sure that God who began the good work within you will keep right on helping you grow in his grace until his task within you is finally finished on that day when Jesus Christ returns."*

This verse sounds like we have not arrived, that something is missing. Are you saved or are you being saved, as it says in another Bible passage?

Again, it becomes necessary to look at the whole of Scripture to understand the truth. Sometimes that takes the form of serious questions about which to pray, study, and ask in the confidence of a trusted mentor or Christian friend. You will find that being born into the Kingdom of God is like being born a US citizen, it is your position with respect to each respective kingdom. However, the way you live each day determines your condition with respect to who you are. As a child of God (your position) you continue to practice what that means each day (your condition). In the same way that you attend school and learn about the foundations of your country and what is expected of you as a responsible citizen, you will also attend worship service, study God's Word and live in the community of other believers where you grow and contribute to the general welfare.

Once we understand our position with God we are able to function freely in His Kingdom. We no longer find it necessary to follow the rules to win points or avoid punishment, but we can do so out of gratitude and love for our new king. We also know that since He was here on earth and overcame temptations, He can understand our weaknesses and is willing to cut us a break when we fall short. It becomes our joy to be more like Him, to overcome obstacles in our relationship with Him and to live in harmony with fellow believers as He has made it clear that we are to do. You are saved because of what God has done, but you are in the process of being saved by living in obedience to His commands.

Questions:

1. In the past, what did you think you had to do to get to heaven? (If you never thought about it that is an answer as well).

2. How has that thinking changed?

3. Since you are already saved why is it important to obey God's commands?

Further reading – Pilgrim's Progress, John Bunyan

STUDY 12 - WHAT DOES THE FUTURE HOLD?

Day 1 - Jesus is Coming Again
Read: Mathew 24:23-47

Jesus attended synagogue regularly. In Luke 4:17 He was handed the book of the prophet Isaiah to read. He found the place where it was written,

> *"The Spirit of the Lord is upon me, because he has anointed me to proclaim good news to the poor. He has sent me to proclaim liberty to the captives and recovering of sight to the blind, to set at liberty those who are oppressed, to proclaim the year of the Lord's favor...."*

He closed the scroll, handed it back to the attendant, and sat down. Everybody was staring at him because he stopped reading in the middle of a sentence. Then He said to them,

> *"This day the scripture is fulfilled in your hearing."*

Apparently, the reason he stopped in the middle of the sentence was the last phrase,

> *"and the day of vengeance of the Lord,"*

which had not yet been fulfilled. The old Testament prophecies telling of Jesus' coming made no distinction between the first coming to redeem, and the second coming to judge, as being at different times. This was confusing to the people of His day because they were looking for the Messiah to free them from Roman domination and establish His rule over the nations. They failed to understand that He would establish His rule of the nations at His second coming. This is much the same as those today who are confused over Jesus' second coming in judgement and His coming in the clouds to catch-up the church.

In the first chapter of the book of Acts we read about the resurrected Christ and His departure from earth. He told the disciples that the time for Him to return and restore the Kingdom of Israel was not for them to know. As He was taken up into a cloud and out of sight, an angel told them that He will come again just as they saw Him go. As you read in the text for today, no one knows the day and hour of His coming. We are told that He will come unexpectedly, at least the world won't be expecting Him to come. However, the believers will be able to discern the signs of the times and will not be surprised on that day of His return.

You will often see bumper stickers proclaiming that Jesus is coming again. I saw a humorous one that said, "Look busy, Jesus is coming." The Israelites had been taught to expect the Messiah to come, but most of them failed to accept Jesus because He didn't fulfill their expectations. This was due to several reasons, one being that Jesus didn't come to free them from Roman oppression. Another reason was that most of their leadership did not accept Jesus. They were expecting somebody with Rabbinic credentials, somebody who would come in power and majesty, somebody who would support their roles and uphold their positions of power. There is a lesson to be learned from their mistake.

We need to be sure that we do not have a false expectation of His coming. He said He was coming to set the captives free and to proclaim the acceptable day of the Lord. When He came the first time it was as a suffering servant. When He comes again He will come as a mighty warrior to wage war with the world order. We are not told to meet Him at any special place, but we are told to be ready. This means we are to continue carrying out His commands to love one another and take the Gospel unto all the world. We do not need to worry about recognizing Him. He said, *"My sheep will know my voice."* Verse 31 says He will send His angels to the four corners of the earth to gather together His elect. His angels will find us! What a comforting thought that we belong to Him and He will seek and find us where we are.

Questions:

1. What changes need to be made in the way you live so you can have confidence about the Lord's return?

2. What false expectations have you held about the return of Jesus?

Day 2 - Why Heaven?
Read: Acts 1:9-11

We all are interested in the future, where we shall live, will we have enough money and when we shall die. Some people read horoscopes or go to fortune tellers to get an idea of what is in store for them. In the Old Testament God warns the Israelites not to seek the counsel of these spiritualists. God wants us to rely upon Him and He knows that it is damaging to us to know the future. What if you were told that you would die before your next birthday? It would change the way you live and you would be unhappy about the prospect of impending death. However, we all have the terminal disease known as life. Knowing that this life is only for a little while we should be especially interested in eternity. The disciples asked about the future, James and John were making plans for it. Jesus spoke often about it. Most everybody wants a utopian existence and many think it is achievable by mankind improving life here on earth. It seems that everybody wants to go to heaven but nobody wants to die.

From the descriptions in the Bible we know that heaven is a good place for us to go because God dwells there. In Dueteronomy 26:15, Moses urges the people to pray to God, asking Him to

"Look down from heaven, your holy dwelling place, and bless your people..."

In 2 Chronicles 30:27 it says,
"Then the priests and Levites stood and blessed the people, and God heard their prayer from his holy dwelling in heaven."

In John 14:2, Jesus says,
"In my Father's house are many mansions; if it were not so I would have told you. I am going to prepare a place for you."

In Acts 1 Jesus is described as ascending up out of sight into the clouds. As earthly creatures we are limited in our understanding.

Since we think in terms of time and space we think of heaven as some physical place, especially up in the sky. We even refer to the sky as heaven. Since we can't comprehend anything that doesn't consist of matter, of being without beginning or end, it is difficult to explain heaven to us. That is why Jesus speaks of heaven being a mansion or that heaven is "up there." Nothing on earth can be compared to heaven. It consists simply and wonderfully of God's presence forever. It isn't necessary for us to know where heaven is, just that God is there and it will be a place far better than anything we have known on earth.

Another way to look at heaven was described by a doctor. His dog was in a room on the other side of a closed door. The dog could hear him and knew he was on the other side of the door. The dog was barking and jumping at the door, wanting to get into the room with his master.

The dog didn't know anything about what the room on the other side was like, only that his master was there and he wanted to be with him. Simply stated, when we go to heaven we will be with our Master forever. That should be good enough for us and nothing else should matter. I dreamed one night that God gave me a task to count. I don't know what it was that I was counting, I just remember how elated I was to be doing something that God wanted done!

"No eye has seen, no ear has heard, and no mind has imagined what God has prepared for those who love him. But God has revealed them to us through His Spirit. For the Spirit searches all things, yes, the deep things of God." 1 Corinthians. 2:9-10.

Questions:

1. What are your expectations of heaven?

2. How does it make you feel to know that Jesus is preparing a place for you in heaven?

3. Do you know Jesus well enough to be satisfied with no more than His presence? If not, make it a goal to know him better.

Day 3 - How Do We Get There?

Read: Mathew 7:13-14

There are many questions about the significance of dreams. We are told in the Old Testament that God appeared to people in dreams, but we have to be careful not to get caught up into dreams and their interpretation. On the other hand, I have found that some dreams are extraordinary, dramatic and memorable. The message from them seems to be too clear to be dismissed. By applying God's Word and asking for His understanding I believe it is possible to get direction or reinforcement through such dreams.

One of my dreams in particular, was about a large group of people gathered around three long ponds of water, like the reflection pools near the Washington Monument. Between these ponds were two concrete dividers, one leading to a large archway and the other to a very small one through which one must crawl. Everybody was being urged to pass along the dividers and through one of the two doors. Most of the crowd was in front of the large archway. The word was being passed among family and friends to choose the smaller opening. It gave me a good feeling knowing I wasn't following the big crowd to the large opening. Since this dream was so vivid and in complete compliance with the Word of God, I take it to be a confirmation that with my family I am walking on the correct pathway to heaven.

Jesus also told us that it is easier for a camel to go through the needle's eye than for a rich man to enter the Kingdom of God. But immediately after that he said. *"The things that are impossible with man are possible with God."* It is believed that Jesus was referring to a well-known opening in the city wall through which a man could pass but not a horse or camel. Nevertheless, He wasn't condemning the money of the rich man, he was telling us that we often allow the material things of life to get in the way of our relationship with God and our fellow man. He also said that any part that causes us to sin should be plucked out and cast away for it is better to live this life without these important body parts than to spend eternity in hell (Matthew 18:9). This is another way to tell us how important it is to avoid all forms of evil. Thanks be to God that our sins are washed away by the blood of Jesus. Otherwise we wouldn't have any body parts left to cast away.

We have previously covered such things as salvation by grace and our position with God versus our condition in Him. It should be clear that we are not saved by doing good works. Instead, we have been saved to do good works. We also know that our works demonstrate our position with God. If the works are not there, perhaps we never fully surrendered our lives to Him. Jesus said in Matthew 7:16, *"By their fruit you will recognize them. Do people pick grapes from thorn bushes, or figs from thistles?"* Our lives should show the results of Christ living in us.

Questions and activities:

1. How would you describe the way to get to heaven?

2. How have the material things in life kept you apart from God?

3. Have you had a significant dream that you believe is a message from God? If so, discuss this with your mentor.

Day 4 - Visions of Heaven
Read: Revelation 21

The Chronicles of Narnia are a series of children's books written by C.S. Lewis. The stories offer many analogies illustrating God's truth. The latter part of *The Last Battle* describes visions of heaven as offered by Mr. Lewis. When the characters in the story arrived in heaven they found beautiful green grass, colorful flowers, and fruit laden trees everywhere. The breeze was refreshing and the sunlight perfect. They were encouraged repeatedly to come, "Further up and further in. The further in you go, the bigger everything gets. The inside is larger than the outside." As they ran without tiring they came upon new wonders and met people they had known from the past. Everyone was in the prime of life.

All of us have questions about heaven. Various passages in the Old Testament describe death as being "joined unto our people," suggesting that we will be reunited with all the faithful family members who have gone before us. However, we wonder how we will feel about loved ones who are not there, whether our beloved pets will be there, whether we will eat and drink, how will we recognize each other, and what age will we be? There are no direct answers to most of these questions, but we can glean a lot of information from Scripture. Revelation 21:1 tells us there will be a new heaven and a new earth, that there will be no sea. There will be no need of the sun or moon, as God will give continuous light so it is fair to believe our glorified bodies will not require sleep. All defects and weaknesses of our bodies will be made well and our bodies will not grow tired or weary. In the fourth verse it says God will wipe away every tear, there will be no more death, nor sorrow, nor crying or pain. We will also receive rewards (crowns) for our faithfulness. Surely we can trust God that heaven will be more wonderful than we can imagine with the limited understanding of our mortality.

The most frequent question asked about heaven is what will happen to the people who never heard the Gospel or "good" people who have not accepted Jesus. In a previous devotion we learned that only God is the judge of who is good. Most importantly, we do not get to heaven by doing good works, it is by the grace of God. With that in mind we have to trust God to be the fair and righteous judge. We do know that those who practice the sins described in Galatians 5:19-21 will not be there. Such people who want nothing to do with God now would never be happy in heaven. Those who do not want to live for God in this world make a conscious decision to separate from Him. How could those who reject God and practice sinning on earth be happy in heaven? Some people like to think that everyone will go to heaven, since God is love He cannot condemn anyone to the eternal torment of hell. Perhaps they are right. Can you imagine how miserable these people would be if forced to spend eternity in a place where God is in complete control and they will not be able to sin? They will be condemned to listening to church music. The truth is, God will not force Himself on us either in this life or the next.

The fact that God in His grace and love can be trusted to save those whose hearts are right is described in Matthew 8:5-13. Although a gentile, this Roman officer loved his servants. He knew who Jesus was and understood His authority in spiritual matters. Matthew says Jesus was amazed by his faith and healed his servant without even going to him.

Going back to *The Last Battle,* we find a similar illustration of the same truth. The characters in the story were surprised to meet in heaven a warrior of the enemy who fought against them. Further inquiry revealed that he had been accepted in heaven because he hated deceitfulness, he was offended when told that all the gods were alike and to serve one was to serve them all. He was of noble character and sought to know the truth but had been deceived into serving the wrong god. When he met the true God he expected to be justly condemned, but he wasn't because he was of sincere and honest heart.

Questions:

1. What questions do you have about heaven?

2. Are you ready to trust God with the future even though everything is not explained to you?

3. Why do you suppose nobody knows all the details about eternity and heaven?

4. Do fictional stories such as *The Last Battle* help you understand more clearly the truth of God's Word?

5. Will you allow unanswered questions to keep you from knowing and following the Lord?

Day 5 - Marriage Supper of the Lamb
Read: Revelation 19:7-9

Food and eating play a vital role in our lives and are often used by God to celebrate special events; reminding us of His faithfulness. God gave instructions to Adam on what to eat in the garden of Eden. He provided food for the Israelites during the Exodus and gave them food rules (kosher) to protect heir health before those health hazards were discovered by science. He established the Passover meal to celebrate the Exodus from Egypt. Jesus performed His first miracle creating wine at a wedding feast. He told parables about eating, fed the 5,000 and then 4,000. In the Passover celebration during the Last Supper with His disciples He established the communion memorial of is sacrificial death, eating His body and drinking His blood.

We know that eating is necessary to sustain our physical bodies; it is an accepted part of our mortal life on earth. As we have seen from the examples above, eating together also has a spiritual significance. We are told both to receive food with thanksgiving and to fast. Our use of food becomes an act of worship. Eating together is a time for connecting in our busy and diverse schedules. Family meals foster warmth, security and love. During meals we receive a sense of belonging that can be a unifying experience for all. Family mealtime is the perfect opportunity to help us learn to function as a team, submit to common family priorities; even learn to practice appropriate manners. Research shows that teenagers who eat dinner four or more times per week with their families have higher academic performance compared with teenagers who eat with their families two or fewer times per week. Frequent family dinners (five or more a week), are associated with lower rates of smoking, drinking, and illegal drug use in pre-teens and teenagers when compared to families who eat together two or fewer times per week. On the other hand, food obsession can have the opposite effect leading to bulimia, anorexia or obesity. When obsessed with food we become focused on the food rather than the provider. Paul instructs us that eating and drinking should be done to the glory of God

The question here is more than the significance of food in our physical lives, but whether we will continue eating and drinking in heaven. In 1 Corinthians 15, Paul tells us we will receive glorified bodies in the resurrection. Will these bodies require food? Consuming food leads to questions about where the food will come from and where will the waste go? Will animals have to be killed for meat? It is difficult to imagine that there will be toilets and sewer systems in heaven. Nobody has the answer to such conjecture, but we can trust that God will provide in a wonderful and glorious way.

Scripture appears to indicate we will continue to eat after the resurrection, that receiving food will continue to be a means of fellowshipping together. Perhaps our glorified bodies will have no waste. God is certainly capable of providing the best of foods through His creative power. In the series *Left Behind* the food simply appeared when needed. One could argue that the reference to the Wedding Feast of the Lamb is figurative, and it may be, but we have many other Scriptures that refer to eating and drinking in heaven. In Matthew 26:29

> *"Jesus said, I will not drink wine again until I drink it new with you in my Father's Kingdom."*

Jesus prepared food for the disciples after His resurrection.

To prove He had a body and was not a ghost He ate a fish. In Isaiah 25:6, the prophet is describing heaven when he says,

> *"In Jerusalem, the Lord of Heaven's Armies will spread a wonderful feast for all the people of the world. It will be a delicious banquet with clear, well aged wine and choice meat."*
> *(NLT)*

Although this is one of those non-essential topics, it was included here to give insight about the future for you as a child of God. The important truth to take away is that God has a plan for us, that we should not get focused on the material things, but on Him as the giver and sustainer of life. We want to honor Him and trust Him with every aspect of this life and the eternal life to come. We should enjoy the food He supplies and use it wisely, thankful for His daily provision.

Questions:

1. Do you enjoy eating a meal with friends and family?

2. What were the dining practices of your family while you were growing up?

3. What were/are the practices you observe in your own home?

4. What changes will you seek to make as a result of this devotion?

5. Are you looking forward to the provisions God is making for you to spend eternity in heaven?

Day 6 - End Times
Read: Matthew 24: 3-44

In about 1967 I was working overtime in Dayton, Ohio. The job required me to wait 15 minutes between each process step. As I waited I was reading from Revelation as part of a Bible study of the end times (eschatology). As I sat at a table, the lamp above started moving back and forth. Then the table seemed to be shaking as well. I realized everything was shaking around me in accordance with a low rumbling sound. I stood up and looked out the window, fully expecting to see Jesus coming to get me. The most interesting part of this experience, a rare but mild earthquake in the Midwest, was that the only thing on my mind was meeting Jesus. I didn't think about my family, my house or any possessions, only to see the Lord coming for me.

Many of us want to know what God's plan is for the future and how the world will end. There is much dispute among the best of scholars about the details and timing, but the Bible is pretty clear on major events. It also says that we should be aware of the signs of the times, those events that will precede the end. Actually, one needs to realize that we will enter the end times, a process that may take place over our lifetime, so we may not see the whole story unfold from start to finish. Since you have been studying God's Word for more than eleven weeks, I trust you are ready for this rather complicated lesson.

The description of the end that is given in the Gospels is not as complete as it is in Revelation. However, the order of events in Revelation are not chronological, which leaves much to speculation and interpretation. One of the most contentious subjects is called the "rapture." Critics will say that the word "rapture" is not in the Bible, and that is essentially correct. But the event is described in I Thessalonians 4:17 where it says,

"Those who are alive and remain will be caught up..."

The Latin word used for "caught up" is raptus. The word rapture was first used in 1909 by English scholar Dr. C.I. Scofield to describe the sudden departure of believers at the coming of the Lord to take the church out of the world. Jesus describes this event in verses 30-31 of today's reading. The description is the same in Mark 13: 24-27 and Luke 21:25-28. All three of these passages and I Thessalonians 4:13-18, refer to Jesus coming in the clouds and gathering the believers. In fact, the Thessalonian passage describes us as rising up to meet Him in the air. Whether this happens before the tribulation, in the middle of the tribulation or after, isn't very important. The point is we should be seeking Him daily and ready to meet Him at all times.

In the book of Revelation we read that a powerful leader (the beast) will rule the world and a false prophet will lead the apostate (false) church, requiring everybody to worship the beast. All the people of the earth will have to worship the beast to receive a mark in their hand or their forehead, without which they cannot buy or sell in the marketplace. With the use of debit cards and the ability to imbed microchips under the skin this begins to look like fulfillment of prophesy in the very near future.

The Bible also tells us there will be a Great Tribulation, a time of terrible upheaval and persecution on the earth that is expected to last seven years. There will be a series of plagues bringing misery to all who worship the beast. Sometime by the end of the tribulation the believers will be caught up to meet the Lord in the air. After this Jesus will come and make war with the beast and his followers. The beast and the false prophet will be captured and thrown alive into the lake of fire. After that an angel will chain Satan in the bottomless pit for 1,000 years during which time the priests of God and of Christ will reign with Him.

At the end of the 1,000 years Satan will be released. He will again deceive the nations and surround God's people in Jerusalem. Fire will come down from heaven and destroy the army of Satan. He will be thrown into the lake of fire with the beast and the false prophet. The dead will all come to life and stand before the great white throne where God will sit in judgment. All whose names not in the Book of Life will be thrown into the lake of fire. There will be a new heaven and new earth. The new Jerusalem will come down out of heaven and we all will live with God for eternity.

You might call this the end of the world in five minutes. I am sure there will be some who will disagree with this feeble attempt to describe the end times, but I hope it will give you an idea of what things are to come and a desire to study eschatology in greater depth. The most important message of prophecy is to remain faithful, that God is in control and has already won the battle against Satan.

Questions:

1. In what way does the description of the end disturb you and in what ways are you comforted?

2. Is there more you would like to know about the end times?

3. Are you prepared to die rather than worship a world leader?

Day 7 - What Next?

No Reading For Today.

Congratulations! You have reached the end of this twelve-week study series. Hopefully, this has been a rewarding time for you as you have grown in your understanding and practice of God's Word. Perhaps it was through these devotionals that you came to Christ. We trust that this series has also caused you to develop a habit of daily devotions. Maybe it has pricked your interest in some of the other suggested reading such as the *Chronicles of Narnia* or *Pilgrim's Progress*. Books like these can help immensely in understanding the application of God's Word and plans for daily living.

Where do you go from here? Today you begin another phase in following Jesus. As you met with your mentor you should have developed plans for moving forward. Each new day brings you closer to living with Jesus in this life, but also in the life to come. Today is the first day in the rest of your life and tomorrow may be the last. It is a time to move on to a new devotional series. *Our Daily Bread* is an excellent devotional, but there are others as well. Ask your mentor to help you get one.

If you started to read through the Bible as a result of this study you are well on the way to completing it. If you were incarcerated and working with a mentor, you are likely out of jail and will be continuing to meet together. You should be working through the plans you made with your mentor and know what is next on your agenda. Hopefully, you are regularly attending worship service and are becoming involved in a small group fellowship. You should also be looking for, or have found a place to serve in the Kingdom of God. If you are working and have an income, you should be managing your money and setting aside a portion for the Lord.

My oldest son is interested in Harley Davidson motorcycles. He buys shirts, belts and other clothing with Harley Davidson logos on them. Even his dog's collar has Harley Davidson on it. This shows his interest to other people and helps him identify with those of like interest. Therefore, it is important what you show of yourself to others. Whether you like it or not, people will judge you by your appearance, actions and language. Actually, the combination of these three characteristics will tell much about who you are, how much you care about yourself and what you want others to think of you. As a child of God you should carefully consider the image you are projecting for others to see.

How are you using your time? Where do you spend your time? On what do you spend your money? All of these are clues about what is important in your life and who you are. As was discussed in the study of inventory, carefully examine these aspects of your life and bring them under submission to God, because that is how others will know you belong to Him. Sometimes it is your "silent" witness that says more than the words from your mouth.

Go with God, remain faithful to Him, and may your future be as bright as the noonday sun.

No more questions

APPENDIX I

The plan of salvation is presented in the book of Romans. It is referred to as the Roman Road.

__First__ we see that we are all guilty before God. In **Romans 1:20-21** we are told:

> *"For since the creation of the world His (God's) invisible attributes are clearly seen, being understood by the things that are made, even His eternal power and Godhead, so that they are without excuse, because, although they knew God, they did not glorify Him as God, nor were thankful, but became futile in their thoughts, and their foolish hearts were darkened."*

Again in **Romans 3:23** we learn

> *"For all have sinned, and fall short of the glory of God."*

We have been born into a fallen world. We have sinned in thought, word and deed by those things we have done and what we have failed to do.

__Next__ we see that the penalty of sin is eternal death. **Romans 6:23a** says,

> *"For the wages of sin is death..."*

When God told Adam and Eve they would die if they ate from the forbidden tree, He was not talking about physical death but the eternal death of our souls. We are hopelessly lost. Hopeless because there isn't anything we can do to undo the curse of sin within us.

However, the verse goes on to say,

> *"But the gift of God is eternal life through Jesus Christ our Lord."*

God has made a way! As described back in **Romans 5:8** where it says,

> *"But God demonstrates His love toward us, in that, while we were still sinners, Christ died for us."*

Without Jesus we were hopeless because we are powerless to remove our sin and save ourselves. Our sin separates us from God and the only means of removing it is the sacrifice of a perfect life. When Jesus died on the cross He paid the penalty for sin. He paid the price for all sin, even ours, when He took all the sins of the world on Himself at the cross, He bought us out of slavery to sin and death! This is called redemption.

Now, the provision has been made for our salvation but something is still missing. We have to be willing to receive it! We have to agree with God about our condition and His provision. Romans 10:9-10 says,

> *".... if you confess with your mouth the Lord Jesus and believe in your heart that God has raised Him from the dead, you will be saved. For with the heart one believes unto righteousness, and with the mouth confession is made unto salvation."*

> *Romans 10:13 "For whosoever calls on the name of the LORD shall be saved."*

All you have to do is call upon the name of the Lord and you will be saved! You can do this right now by prayer. God knows the attitude of your heart and is not concerned about the words. You can pray a prayer of your own or simply repeat the following suggested prayer:

Almighty Father; I enter Your presence confessing the things I try to conceal from You and the things I try to conceal from others. I confess the heartbreak, worry, and sorrow I have caused, that make it difficult for others to forgive me, the times I have led others astray, the harm I have done that makes it hard for me to forgive myself.

I know I am not deserving of Your mercy and grace, but I also realize that You still love me and want to change the way I have been living. I invite Jesus to come into my heart and change the way I think. Transform my mind and give me a new heart. Let my life be pleasing and acceptable in Your sight. I know I will not always do right, but I invite You to expose every wrongdoing so that I may confess it and continue to receive Your blessings.

Amen.

You were sin's slave, but now *you are a child of God!*

Tell your mentor about the decision you have made and make plans to be baptized and continue following in Jesus' steps.

APPENDIX II

Translations

The Bible had to be translated from the original text in Hebrew and

Greek to other languages. A translation is not the same as a paraphrase. A translation is an attempt to use words from the new language to express the same ideas of the old language. A good example is the word "hope." To our culture this word expresses wishful thinking, but a more accurate meaning would be "expectation." A paraphrase of the Bible is an attempt by the writer to express the words and ideas according to his understanding. Paraphrases are not always accurate since the writer often twists the words to match his personal bias. The *Message* (MSG) is a paraphrase.

You will find a number of Bible translations. If you have a King James Version you may want to get a *New King James* (NKJ), the *New International Version* (NIV), or the *Living New Testament* (LNT). The LNT is an accurate translation that is easy to read and understand. It is often found in *The Life Application and Study* version with commentary to help explain things.

Bible Structure

The Bible is divided into two parts, the **Old Testament** and the **New Testament**. Each of these is further divided up into **Books**, **Chapters** and **Verses**. Numbering the verses is intended as a universal reference system. For example, "I John 1:13-16" is the first book of John, the first chapter, verses 13 thru 16. One must learn that first John is an **epistle** (letter) that is followed by second and third John. There is also the Gospel of John that is not numbered with the epistles. This may sound pretty confusing right now but with time it will begin to make sense.

The Old Testament

These are the books prior to the coming of Jesus. The Old Testament has 39 books telling the story of the creation and the relationship of God to man that gives us the Jewish history of faith.

The main theme is the coming of the Messiah or the Christ. Apart from the Old and New Testaments, the Bible is not necessarily arranged in the order by which things happened. A Bible read through plan is in Appendix III

Books 1-5: Genesis, Exodus, Leviticus, Numbers, Deuteronomy. These books were written perhaps as long as 3400 years ago, by Moses. These five books are sometimes called the Pentateuch or the Torah.

Books 6-16: Joshua, Judges, Ruth, 1 Samuel, 2 Samuel, 1 Kings, 2 Kings, 1 Chronicles, 2 Chronicles, Ezra, Nehemiah. These books explain the history of Israel from the time the nation was established about 3400 years ago. It includes information about the time when the nation was conquered by the Assyrians about 2700 years ago, and when it was conquered by the Babylonians about 2600 years ago. The Assyrians and Babylonians forced the Jews out of their homeland. But, many Jews returned during the next few centuries, shortly before the time of Jesus.

Books 17-22: Ester, Job, Psalms, Proverbs, Ecclesiastes, Song of Solomon. These books are sometimes called the books of Writings, or the books of Poetry, or the books of Wisdom.

Books 23-27: Isaiah, Jeremiah, Lamentations, Ezekiel, Daniel. These books are called the "major" prophets and contain prophecies delivered by Isaiah, Jeremiah, Ezekiel and Daniel. These prophets lived about 2700 to 2500 years ago. Some of their prophecies found fulfillment more than 2500 years ago. Christians believe that many of the prophecies were fulfilled by Jesus about 2000 years ago.

Books 28-39: Hosea, Joel, Amos, Obadiah, Jonah, Micah, Nahum, Habakkuk, Zephaniah, Haggai, Zechariah, Malachi. These books are sometimes called the books of the "minor" prophets. They are called "minor" because their books are short in length.

The Catholic Old Testament contains some additional books commonly referred to as Apocrypha. Four hundred years pass between the last writings of the Old Testament prophets and John the Baptist.

The New Testament

These are the books written about Jesus and the birth of the early Christian Church. The New Testament has 27 books.

Books 1-4: Matthew, Mark, Luke and John. These four books are called the Gospels (Good News). They were written about 2000 years ago by the followers of Jesus. These books contain details about the life and teachings of Jesus Christ. Some "red letter" editions show the words of Jesus in red type.

Books 5-26: Acts, Romans, 1 Corinthians, 2 Corinthians, Galatians,

Ephesians, Philippians, Colossians, 1 Thessalonians, 2 Thessalonians, 1

Timothy, 2 Timothy, Titus, Philemon, Hebrews, James, 1 Peter, 2 Peter,

1 John, 2 John, 3 John, Jude. These 22 books are sometimes called Letters or Epistles. They were written by followers of Jesus. They often were sent to other people to help explain Christianity. Sometimes they were written to counter heresy, or wrongful interpretations of the teachings of Jesus.

Book 27: Revelation.

This book was written by the apostle John about 1900 years ago. He was shown visions of the future by Jesus. This book contains many prophecies about the End Times.

APPENDIX III

JAN	BIBLE READ THROUGH			√
1	Luke 5:27-39	Genesis 1-2	Psalm 1	
2	Luke 6:1-26	Genesis 3-5	Psalm 2	
3	Luke 6:27-49	Genesis 6-7	Psalm 3	
4	Luke 7:1-17	Genesis 8-10	Psalm 4	
5	Luke 7:18-50	Genesis 11	Psalm 5	
6	Luke 8:1-25	Genesis 12	Psalm 6	
7	Luke 8:26-56	Genesis 13-14	Psalm 7	
8	Luke 9:1-27	Genesis 15	Psalm 8	
9	Luke 9:28-62	Genesis 16	Psalm 9	
10	Luke 10:1-20	Genesis 17	Psalm 10	
11	Luke 10:21-42	Genesis 18	Psalm 11	
12	Luke 11:1-28	Genesis 19	Psalm 12	
13	Luke 11:29-54	Genesis 20	Psalm 13	
14	Luke 12:1-31	Genesis 21	Psalm 14	
15	Luke 12:32-59	Genesis 22	Psalm 15	

16	Luke 13:1-17	Genesis 23	Psalm 16	
17	Luke 13:18-35	Genesis 24	Psalm 17	
18	Luke 14:1-24	Genesis 25	Psalm 18	
19	Luke 14:25-35	Genesis 26	Psalm 19	
20	Luke 15	Genesis 27:1-45	Psalm 20	
21	Luke 16	Genesis 27:4628:22	Psalm 21	
22	Luke 17	Genesis 29:1-30	Psalm 22	
23	Luke 18:1-17	Genesis 29:3130:43	Psalm 23	
24	Luke 18:18-43	Genesis 31	Psalm 24	
25	Luke 19:1-27	Genesis 32-33	Psalm 25	
26	Luke 19:28-48	Genesis 34	Psalm 26	
27	Luke 20:1-26	Genesis 35-36	Psalm 27	
28	Luke 20:27-47	Genesis 37	Psalm 28	
29	Luke 21	Genesis 38	Psalm 29	
30	Luke 22:1-38	Genesis 39	Psalm 30	
31	Luke 22:39-71	Genesis 40	Psalm 31	

FEB	BIBLE READ THROUGH			√
1	Luke 23:1-25	Genesis 41	Psalm 32	
2	Luke 23:26-56	Genesis 42	Psalm 33	
3	Luke 24:1-12	Genesis 43	Psalm 34	
4	Luke 24:13-53	Genesis 44	Psalm 35	
5	Hebrews 1	Genesis 45:1-46:27	Psalm 36	
6	Hebrews 2	Genesis 46:28-47:31	Psalm 37	
7	Hebrews 3:1-4:13	Genesis 48	Psalm 38	
8	Hebrews 4:14-6:12	Genesis 49-50	Psalm 39	
9	Hebrews 6:13-20	Exodus 1-2	Psalm 40	
10	Hebrews 7	Exodus 3-4	Psalm 41	
11	Hebrews 8	Exodus 5:1-6:27	Proverbs 1	
12	Hebrews 9:1-22	Exodus 6:28-8:32	Proverbs 2	
13	Hebrews 9:2310:18	Exodus 9-10	Proverbs 3	
14	Hebrews 10:19-39	Exodus 11-12	Proverbs 4	

15	Hebrews 11:1-22	Exodus 13-14	Proverbs 5	
16	Hebrews 11:23-40	Exodus 15	Proverbs 6:17:5	
17	Hebrews 12	Exodus 16-17	Proverbs 7:6-27	
18	Hebrews 13	Exodus 18-19	Proverbs 8	
19	Matthew 1	Exodus 20-21	Proverbs 9	
20	Matthew 2	Exodus 22-23	Proverbs 10	
21	Matthew 3	Exodus 24	Proverbs 11	
22	Matthew 4	Exodus 25-27	Proverbs 12	
23	Matthew 5:1-20	Exodus 28-29	Proverbs 13	
24	Matthew 5:21-48	Exodus 30-32	Proverbs 14	
25	Matthew 6:1-18	Exodus 33-34	Proverbs 15	
26	Matthew 6:19-34	Exodus 35-36	Proverbs 16	
27	Matthew 7	Exodus 37-38	Proverbs 17	
28	Matthew 8:1-13	Exodus 39-40	Proverbs 18	
MAR	**BIBLE READ THROUGH**			√
1	Matthew 8:14-34	Leviticus 1-2	Proverbs 19	

2	Matthew 9:1-17	Leviticus 3-4	Proverbs 20	
3	Matthew 9:18-38	Leviticus 5-6	Proverbs 21	
4	Matthew 10:1-25	Leviticus 7-8	Proverbs 22	
5	Matthew 10:26-42	Leviticus 9-10	Proverbs 23	
6	Matthew 11:1-19	Leviticus 11-12	Proverbs 24	
7	Matthew 11:20-30	Leviticus 13	Proverbs 25	
8	Matthew 12:1-21	Leviticus 14	Proverbs 26	
9	Matthew 12:22-50	Leviticus 15-16	Proverbs 27	
10	Matthew 13:1-23	Leviticus 17-18	Proverbs 28	
11	Matthew 13:24-58	Leviticus 19	Proverbs 29	
12	Matthew 14:1-21	Leviticus 20-21	Proverbs 30	
13	Matthew 14:22-36	Leviticus 22-23	Proverbs 31	
14	Matthew 15:1-20	Leviticus 24-25	Ecclesiastes 1:111	
15	Matthew 15:21-39	Leviticus 26-27	Ecc. 1:12-2:26	
16	Matthew 16	Numbers 1-2	Ecc. 3:1-15	
17	Matthew 17	Numbers 3-4	Ecc. 3:16-4:16	

18	Matthew 18:1-20	Numbers 5-6	Ecclesiastes 5	
19	Matthew 18:21-35	Numbers 7-8	Ecclesiastes 6	
20	Matthew 19:1-15	Numbers 9-10	Ecclesiastes 7	
21	Matthew 19:16-30	Numbers 11-12	Ecclesiastes 8	
22	Matthew 20:1-16	Numbers 13-14	Ecc. 9:1-12	
23	Matthew 20:17-34	Numbers 15-16	Ecc. 9:13-10:20	
24	Matthew 21:1-27	Numbers 17-18	Ecc. 11:1-8	
25	Matthew 21:28-46	Numbers 19-20	Ecc. 11:9-12:14	
26	Matthew 22:1-22	Numbers 21	Solomon 1:1-2:7	
27	Matthew 22:23-46	Numbers 22:140	Solomon 2:8-3:5	
28	Matthew 23:1-12	Numbers 22:4123:26	Solomon 3:6-5:1	
29	Matthew 23:13-39	Numbers 23:2724:25	Solomon 5:2-6:3	
30	Matthew 24:1-31	Numbers 25-27	Solomon 6:4-8:4	
31	Matthew 24:32-51	Numbers 28-29	Solomon 8:5-14	

APR	BIBLE READ THROUGH			√
1	Matthew 25:1-30	Numbers 30-31	Job 1	
2	Matthew 25:31-46	Numbers 32-34	Job 2	
3	Matthew 26:1-25	Numbers 35-36	Job 3	
4	Matthew 26:26-46	Deuteronomy 1-2	Job 4	
5	Matthew 26:47-75	Deuteronomy 3-4	Job 5	
6	Matthew 27:1-31	Deuteronomy 5-6	Job 6	
7	Matthew 27:32-66	Deuteronomy 7-8	Job 7	
8	Matthew 28	Deuteronomy 9-10	Job 8	
9	Acts 1	Deuteronomy 11-12	Job 9	
10	Acts 2:1-13	Deuteronomy 13-14	Job 10	
11	Acts 2:14-47	Deuteronomy 15-16	Job 11	
12	Acts 3	Deuteronomy 17-18	Job 12	
13	Acts 4:1-22	Deuteronomy 19-20	Job 13	
14	Acts 4:23-37	Deuteronomy 21-22	Job 14	
15	Acts 5:1-16	Deuteronomy 23-24	Job 15	

16	Acts 5:17-42	Deuteronomy 25-27	Job 16	
17	Acts 6	Deuteronomy 28	Job 17	
18	Acts 7:1-22	Deuteronomy 29-30	Job 18	
19	Acts 7:23-8:1	Deuteronomy 31-32	Job 19	
20	Acts 8:1-25	Deuteronomy 33-34	Job 20	
21	Acts 8:26-40	Joshua 1-2	Job 21	
22	Acts 9:1-25	Joshua 3:1-5:1	Job 22	
23	Acts 9:26-43	Joshua 5:2-6:27	Job 23	
24	Acts 10:1-33	Joshua 7-8	Job 24	
25	Acts 10:34-48	Joshua 9-10	Job 25	
26	Acts 11:1-18	Joshua 11-12	Job 26	
27	Acts 11:19-30	Joshua 13-14	Job 27	
28	Acts 12	Joshua 15-17	Job 28	
29	Acts 13:1-25	Joshua 18-19	Job 29	
30	Acts 13:26-52	Joshua 20-21	Job 30	

MAY	BIBLE READ THROUGH	√

1	Acts 14	Joshua 22	Job 31	
2	Acts 15:1-21	Joshua 23-24	Job 32	
3	Acts 15:22-41	Judges 1	Job 33	
4	Acts 16:1-15	Judges 2-3	Job 34	
5	Acts 16:16-40	Judges 4-5	Job 35	
6	Acts 17:1-15	Judges 6	Job 36	
7	Acts 17:16-34	Judges 7-8	Job 37	
8	Acts 18	Judges 9	Job 38	
9	Acts 19:1-20	Judges 10:1-11:33	Job 39	
10	Acts 19:21-41	Judges 11:34-12:15	Job 40	
11	Acts 20:1-16	Judges 13	Job 41	
12	Acts 20:17-38	Judges 14-15	Job 42	
13	Acts 21:1-36	Judges 16	Psalm 42	
14	Acts 21:37 22:29	Judges 17-18	Psalm 43	
15	Acts 22:30 23:22	Judges 19	Psalm 44	
16	Acts 23:23-24:9	Judges 20	Psalm 45	

17	Acts 24:10-27	Judges 21	Psalm 46	
18	Acts 25	Ruth 1-2	Psalm 47	
19	Acts 26:1-18	Ruth 3-4	Psalm 48	
20	Acts 26:19-32	1 Samuel 1:1-2:10	Psalm 49	
21	Acts 27:1-12	1 Samuel 2:11-36	Psalm 50	
22	Acts 27:13-44	1 Samuel 3	Psalm 51	
23	Acts 28:1-16	1 Samuel 4-5	Psalm 52	
24	Acts 28:17-31	1 Samuel 6-7	Psalm 53	
25	Romans 1:1-15	1 Samuel 8	Psalm 54	
26	Romans 1:16-32	1 Samuel 9:1-10:16	Psalm 55	
27	Romans 2:1-3:8	1 Samuel 10:17-11:15	Psalm 56	
28	Romans 3:9-31	1 Samuel 12	Psalm 57	
29	Romans 4	1 Samuel 13	Psalm 58	
30	Romans 5	1 Samuel 14	Psalm 59	
31	Romans 6	1 Samuel 15	Psalm 60	

JUN	BIBLE READ THROUGH			√
1	Romans 7	1 Samuel 16	Psalm 61	
2	Romans 8	1 Samuel 17:1-54	Psalm 62	
3	Romans 9:1-29	1 Samuel 17:55-18:30	Psalm 63	
4	Romans 9:3010:21	1 Samuel 19	Psalm 64	
5	Romans 11:1-24	1 Samuel 20	Psalm 65	
6	Romans 11:25-36	1 Samuel 21-22	Psalm 66	
7	Romans 12	1 Samuel 23-24	Psalm 67	
8	Romans 13	1 Samuel 25	Psalm 68	
9	Romans 14	1 Samuel 26	Psalm 69	
10	Romans 15:1-13	1 Samuel 27-28	Psalm 70	
11	Romans 15:14-33	1 Samuel 29-31	Psalm 71	
12	Romans 16	2 Samuel 1	Psalm 72	
13	Mark 1:1-20	2 Samuel 2:1-3:1	Daniel 1	
14	Mark 1:21-45	2 Samuel 3:2-39	Daniel 2:1-23	
15	Mark 2	2 Samuel 4-5	Daniel 2:24-49	

16	Mark 3:1-19	2 Samuel 6	Daniel 3	
17	Mark 3:20-35	2 Samuel 7-8	Daniel 4	
18	Mark 4:1-20	2 Samuel 9-10	Daniel 5	
19	Mark 4:21-41	2 Samuel 11-12	Daniel 6	
20	Mark 5:1-20	2 Samuel 13	Daniel 7	
21	Mark 5:21-43	2 Samuel 14	Daniel 8	
22	Mark 6:1-29	2 Samuel 15	Daniel 9	
23	Mark 6:30-56	2 Samuel 16	Daniel 10:1-21	
24	Mark 7:1-13	2 Samuel 17	Daniel 11:1-19	
25	Mark 7:14-37	2 Samuel 18	Daniel 11:20-45	
26	Mark 8:1-21	2 Samuel 19	Daniel 12	
27	Mark 8:22-9:1	2 Samuel 20-21	Hosea 1:1-2:1	
28	Mark 9:2-50	2 Samuel 22	Hosea 2:2-23	
29	Mark 10:1-31	2 Samuel 23	Hosea 3	
30	Mark 10:32-52	2 Samuel 24	Hosea 4:1-11	

JUL	BIBLE READ THROUGH	√

1	Mark 11:1-14	1 Kings 1	Hosea 4:1-5:4	
2	Mark 11:15-33	1 Kings 2	Hosea 5:5-15	
3	Mark 12:1-27	1 Kings 3	Hosea 6:1-7:2	
4	Mark 12:28-44	1 Kings 4-5	Hosea 7:3-16	
5	Mark 13:1-13	1 Kings 6	Hosea 8	
6	Mark 13:14-37	1 Kings 7	Hosea 9:1-16	
7	Mark 14:1-31	1 Kings 8	Hosea 9:17-10:15	
8	Mark 14:32-72	1 Kings 9	Hosea 11:1-11	
9	Mark 15:1-20	1 Kings 10	Hosea 11:12-12:14	
10	Mark 15:21-47	1 Kings 11	Hosea 13	
11	Mark 16	1 Kings 12:1-31	Hosea 14	
12	1 Cor. 1:1-17	1 Kings 12:32-13:34	Joel 1	
13	1 Cor. 1:18-31	1 Kings 14	Joel 2:1-11	
14	1 Corinthians 2	1 Kings 15:1-32	Joel 2:12-32	
15	1 Corinthians 3	1 Kings 15:33-16:34	Joel 3	
16	1 Corinthians 4	1 Kings 17	Amos 1	

17	1 Corinthians 5	1 Kings 18	Amos 2:1-3:2	
18	1 Corinthians 6	1 Kings 19	Amos 3:3-4:3	
19	1 Cor. 7:1-24	1 Kings 20	Amos 4:4-13	
20	1 Cor. 7:25-40	1 Kings 21	Amos 5	
21	1 Corinthians 8	1 Kings 22	Amos 6	
22	1 Corinthians 9	2 Kings 1-2	Amos 7	
23	1 Corinthians 10	2 Kings 3	Amos 8	
24	1 Cor. 11:1-16	2 Kings 4	Amos 9	
25	1 Cor. 11:17-34	2 Kings 5	Obadiah 1	
26	1 Corinthians 12	2 Kings 6:1-7:2	Jonah 1	
27	1 Corinthians 13	2 Kings 7:3-20	Jonah 2	
28	1 Cor. 14:1-25	2 Kings 8	Jonah 3	
29	1 Cor. 14:26-40	2 Kings 9	Jonah 4	
30	1 Cor. 15:1-34	2 Kings 10	Micah 1	
31	1 Cor. 15:35-58	2 Kings 11	Micah 2	

AUG	BIBLE READ THROUGH			√
1	1 Corinthians 16	2 Kings 12-13	Micah 3	
2	2 Cor. 1:1-2:4	2 Kings 14	Micah 4:1-5:1	
3	2 Cor. 2:5-3:18	2 Kings 15-16	Micah 5:2-15	
4	2 Cor. 4:1-5:10	2 Kings 17	Micah 6	
5	2 Cor. 5:11-6:13	2 Kings 18	Micah 7	
6	2 Cor. 6:14-7:16	2 Kings 19	Nahum 1	
7	2 Corinthians 8	2 Kings 20-21	Nahum 2	
8	2 Corinthians 9	2 Kings 22:1-23:35	Nahum 3	
9	2 Corinthians 10	2 Kings 23:36-24:20	Habakkuk 1	
10	2 Corinthians 11	2 Kings 25	Habakkuk 2	
11	2 Corinthians 12	1 Chronicles 1-2	Habakkuk 3	
12	2 Corinthians 13	1 Chronicles 3-4	Zephaniah 1	

13	John 1:1-18	1 Chronicles 5-6	Zephaniah 2	
14	John 1:19-34	1 Chronicles 7-8	Zephaniah 3	
15	John 1:35-51	1 Chronicles 9	Haggai 1-2	
16	John 2	1 Chronicles 10-11	Zechariah 1	
17	John 3:1-21	1 Chronicles 12	Zechariah 2	
18	John 3:22-36	1 Chronicles 13-14	Zechariah 3	
19	John 4:1-26	1 Chron. 15:1-16:6	Zechariah 4	
20	John 4:27-42	1 Chronicles 16:7-43	Zechariah 5	
21	John 4:43-54	1 Chronicles 17	Zechariah 6	
22	John 5:1-18	1 Chronicles 18-19	Zechariah 7	
23	John 5:19-47	1 Chron. 20:1-22:1	Zechariah 8	
24	John 6:1-21	1 Chron. 22:2-23:32	Zechariah 9	
25	John 6:22-59	1 Chronicles 24	Zechariah 10	
26	John 6:60-71	1 Chronicles 25-26	Zechariah 11	
27	John 7:1-24	1 Chronicles 27-28	Zechariah 12	
28	John 7:25-52	1 Chronicles 29	Zechariah 13	

29	John 8:1-20	2 Chronicles 1:1-2:16	Zechariah 14	
30	John 8:21-47	2 Chronicles 2:17-5:1	Malachi 1:12:9	
31	John 8:48-59	2 Chronicles 5:2-14	Malachi 2:1016	

SEP	BIBLE READ THROUGH			√
1	John 9:1-23	2 Chronicles 6	Malachi 2:173:18	
2	John 9:24-41	2 Chronicles 7	Malachi 4	
3	John 10:1-21	2 Chronicles 8	Psalm 73	
4	John 10:22-42	2 Chronicles 9	Psalm 74	
5	John 11:1-27	2 Chronicles 10-11	Psalm 75	
6	John 11:28-57	2 Chronicles 12-13	Psalm 76	
7	John 12:1-26	2 Chronicles 14-15	Psalm 77	
8	John 12:27-50	2 Chronicles 16-17	Psalm 78:1-20	
9	John 13:1-20	2 Chronicles 18	Psalm 78:21-37	
10	John 13:21-38	2 Chronicles 19	Psalm 78:38-55	
11	John 14:1-14	2 Chron. 20:1-21:1	Psalm 78:56-72	

12	John 14:15-31	2 Chron. 21:2-22:12	Psalm 79	
13	John 15:1-16:4a	2 Chronicles 23	Psalm 80	
14	John 16:4b-33	2 Chronicles 24	Psalm 81	
15	John 17	2 Chronicles 25	Psalm 82	
16	John 18:1-18	2 Chronicles 26	Psalm 83	
17	John 18:19-38	2 Chronicles 27-28	Psalm 84	
18	John 18:38b19:16	2 Chronicles 29	Psalm 85	
19	John 19:16-42	2 Chronicles 30	Psalm 86	
20	John 20:1-18	2 Chronicles 31	Psalm 87	
21	John 20:19-31	2 Chronicles 32	Psalm 88	
22	John 21	2 Chronicles 33	Psalm 89:1-18	
23	1 John 1	2 Chronicles 34	Psalm 89:19-37	
24	1 John 2	2 Chronicles 35	Psalm 89:38-52	
25	1 John 3	2 Chronicles 36	Psalm 90	
26	1 John 4	Ezra 1-2	Psalm 91	
27	1 John 5	Ezra 3-4	Psalm 92	

28	2 John	Ezra 5-6	Psalm 93	
29	3 John	Ezra 7-8	Psalm 94	
30	Jude	Ezra 9-10	Psalm 95	

OCT	BIBLE READ THROUGH			√
1	Revelation 1	Nehemiah 1-2	Psalm 96	
2	Revelation 2	Nehemiah 3	Psalm 97	
3	Revelation 3	Nehemiah 4	Psalm 98	
4	Revelation 4	Neh. 5:1-7:4	Psalm 99	
5	Revelation 5	Neh. 7:5-8:12	Psalm 100	
6	Revelation 6	Neh. 8:13-9:37	Psalm 101	
7	Revelation 7	Neh. 9:38-10:39	Psalm 102	
8	Revelation 8	Nehemiah 11	Psalm 103	
9	Revelation 9	Nehemiah 12	Psalm 104:1-23	
10	Revelation 10	Nehemiah 13	Psalm 104:24-35	
11	Revelation 11	Esther 1	Psalm 105:1-25	

12	Revelation 12	Esther 2	Psalm 105:26-45	
13	Revelation 13	Esther 3-4	Psalm 106:1-23	
14	Revelation 14	Esther 5:1-6:13	Psalm 106:24-48	
15	Revelation 15	Esther 6:14-8:17	Psalm 107:1-22	
16	Revelation 16	Esther 9-10	Psalm 107:23-43	
17	Revelation 17	Isaiah 1-2	Psalm 108	
18	Revelation 18	Isaiah 3-4	Psalm 109:1-19	
19	Revelation 19	Isaiah 5-6	Psalm 109:20-31	
20	Revelation 20	Isaiah 7-8	Psalm 110	
21	Rev. 21-22	Isaiah 9-10	Psalm 111	
22	1 Thess. 1	Isaiah 11-13	Psalm 112	
23	1 Thess. 2:1-16	Isaiah 14-16	Psalm 113	
24	1 Thess. 2:17-3:13	Isaiah 17-19	Psalm 114	
25	1 Thess. 4	Isaiah 20-22	Psalm 115	
26	1 Thess. 5	Isaiah 23-24	Psalm 116	
27	2 Thess. 1	Isaiah 25-26	Psalm 117	

28	2 Thess. 2	Isaiah 27-28	Psalm 118	
29	2 Thess. 3	Isaiah 29-30	Psalm 119:1-32	
30	1 Timothy 1	Isaiah 31-33	Psalm 119:33-64	
31	1 Timothy 2	Isaiah 34-35	Psalm 119:65-96	

NOV	BIBLE READ THROUGH			√
1	1 Timothy 3	Isaiah 36-37	Psalm 119:97-120	
2	1 Timothy 4	Isaiah 38-39	Psalm 119:121144	
3	1 Timothy 5:1-22	Jeremiah 1-2	Psalm 119:145176	
4	1 Timothy 5:23-6:21	Jeremiah 3-4	Psalm 120	
5	2 Timothy 1	Jeremiah 5-6	Psalm 121	
6	2 Timothy 2	Jeremiah 7-8	Psalm 122	
7	2 Timothy 3	Jeremiah 9-10	Psalm 123	
8	2 Timothy 4	Jeremiah 11-12	Psalm 124	
9	Titus 1	Jeremiah 13-14	Psalm 125	
10	Titus 2	Jeremiah 15-16	Psalm 126	

11	Titus 3	Jeremiah 17-18	Psalm 127	
12	Philemon	Jeremiah 19-20	Psalm 128	
13	James 1	Jeremiah 21-22	Psalm 129	
14	James 2	Jeremiah 23-24	Psalm 130	
15	James 3	Jeremiah 25-26	Psalm 131	
16	James 4	Jeremiah 27-28	Psalm 132	
17	James 5	Jeremiah 29-30	Psalm 133	
18	1 Peter 1	Jeremiah 31-32	Psalm 134	
19	1 Peter 2	Jeremiah 33-34	Psalm 135	
20	1 Peter 3	Jeremiah 35-36	Psalm 136	
21	1 Peter 4	Jeremiah 37-38	Psalm 137	
22	1 Peter 5	Jeremiah 39-40	Psalm 138	
23	2 Peter 1	Jeremiah 41-42	Psalm 139	
24	2 Peter 2	Jeremiah 43-44	Psalm 140	
25	2 Peter 3	Jeremiah 45-46	Psalm 141	
26	Galatians 1	Jeremiah 47-48	Psalm 142	

27	Galatians 2	Jeremiah 49-50	Psalm 143	
28	Galatians 3:1-18	Jeremiah 51-52	Psalm 144	
29	Galatians 3:19-4:20	Lamentations 1-2	Psalm 145	
30	Galatians 4:21-31	Lamentations 3-4	Psalm 146	

DEC	BIBLE READ THROUGH			√
1	Galatians 5:1-15	Lamentations 5	Psalm 147	
2	Galatians 5:16-26	Ezekiel 1	Psalm 148	
3	Galatians 6	Ezekiel 2-3	Psalm 149	
4	Ephesians 1	Ezekiel 4-5	Psalm 150	
5	Ephesians 2	Ezekiel 6-7	Isaiah 40	
6	Ephesians 3	Ezekiel 8-9	Isaiah 41	
7	Ephesians 4:1-16	Ezekiel 10-11	Isaiah 42	
8	Ephesians 4:17-32	Ezekiel 12-13	Isaiah 43	
9	Ephesians 5:1-20	Ezekiel 14-15	Isaiah 44	
10	Ephesians 5:21-33	Ezekiel 16	Isaiah 45	

11	Ephesians 6	Ezekiel 17	Isaiah 46	
12	Philippians 1:1-11	Ezekiel 18	Isaiah 47	
13	Philippians 1:12-30	Ezekiel 19	Isaiah 48	
14	Philippians 2:1-11	Ezekiel 20	Isaiah 49	
15	Philippians 2:12-30	Ezekiel 21-22	Isaiah 50	
16	Philippians 3	Ezekiel 23	Isaiah 51	
17	Philippians 4	Ezekiel 24	Isaiah 52	
18	Colossians 1:1-23	Ezekiel 25-26	Isaiah 53	
19	Colossians 1:242:19	Ezekiel 27-28	Isaiah 54	
20	Colossians 2:203:17	Ezekiel 29-30	Isaiah 55	
21	Colossians 3:184:18	Ezekiel 31-32	Isaiah 56	
22	Luke 1:1-25	Ezekiel 33	Isaiah 57	
23	Luke 1:26-56	Ezekiel 34	Isaiah 58	
24	Luke 1:57-80	Ezekiel 35-36	Isaiah 59	
25	Luke 2:1-20	Ezekiel 37	Isaiah 60	
26	Luke 2:21-52	Ezekiel 38-39	Isaiah 61	

27	Luke 3:1-20	Ezekiel 40-41	Isaiah 62	
28	Luke 3:21-38	Ezekiel 42-43	Isaiah 63	
29	Luke 4:1-30	Ezekiel 44-45	Isaiah 64	
30	Luke 4:31-44	Ezekiel 46-47	Isaiah 65	
31	Luke 5:1-26	Ezekiel 48	Isaiah 66	

www.ingramcontent.com/pod-product-compliance
Lightning Source LLC
Chambersburg PA
CBHW051137120626
46547CB00012B/840